CULTURES OF THE WORLD

SUDAN

Patricia Levy & Zawiah Abdul Latif

Marshall Cavendish
Benchmark
New York

PICTURE CREDITS
Cover photo: © Jonathan Blair / CORBIS
alt.TYPE / Reuters: 54, 57, 73, 105, 121 • Andes Press Agency: 48, 59, 80, 115 • Susanna Burton: 46, 111 • Focus Team: 1, 17, 20, 82, 128 • Hulton Deutsch: 27 • Hutchison Library: 3, 10, 11, 12, 13, 25, 29, 33, 37, 39, 64, 66, 67, 69, 71, 74, 76, 79, 83, 86, 87, 90, 91, 94, 97, 99, 103, 109, 112, 119, 124, 127 • Image Bank: 16 • Björn Klingwall: 23, 60, 72, 93, 101, 116 • Photolibrary: 6, 8, 46, 50, 63, 100, 114 • Photolibrary / Alamy: 14, 32, 58, 113 • R. Ian Lloyd: 5, 7, 15, 40, 61, 70, 84, 92, 108, 110, 120 • Reuters Visnews Library: 77 • Peter Sanders: 4, 18, 19, 22, 24, 31, 34, 41, 43, 65, 88, 102, 104, 122, 123, 126 • Stockfood: 130, 131 • Liba Taylor: 45, 81

PRECEDING PAGE
Sudanese boys smiling at the camera.

Publisher (U.S.): Michelle Bisson
Editors: Deborah Grahame, Mabelle Yeo, Crystal Ouyang, Janelle Chua
Copyreader: Sherry Chiger
Designers: Jailani Basari, Benson Tan, Rachel Chen
Cover picture researcher: Connie Gardner
Picture researchers: Thomas Khoo, Joshua Ang

Marshall Cavendish Benchmark
99 White Plains Road
Tarrytown, NY 10591
Web site: www.marshallcavendish.us

Originated and designed by Times Editions Private Limited
An imprint of Marshall Cavendish International (Asia) Private Limited
A member of Times Publishing Limited

All Internet sites were correct and accurate at the time of printing. All monetary figures in this publication are in U.S. dollars.

Library of Congress Cataloging-in-Publication Data
Levy, Patricia, 1951–
    Sudan / by Patricia Levy and Zawiah Abdul Latif. — 2nd ed.
      p. cm. — (Cultures of the world)
    Summary: "Provides comprehensive information on the geography, history, wildlife, governmental structure, economy, cultural
      diversity, peoples, religion, and culture of Sudan"—Provided by publisher.
    Includes bibliographical references and index.
      ISBN 978-0-7614-2083-5
    1. Sudan—Juvenile literature. I. Latif, Zawiah Abdul. II. Title. III. Series.
    DT154.6.L48 2007
    962.4—dc22   2006101725

Printed in China

9 8 7 6 5 4 3 2 1

CONTENTS

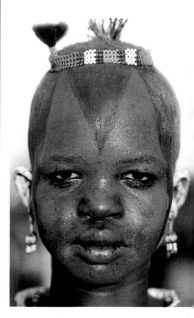

A young girl of the Dinka tribe, with her face painted for a special occasion.

Arabs make up the largest ethnic group in Sudan.

INTRODUCTION

THE PLACE WHERE AFRICAN AND Arab cultures mingle, Sudan is home to a physically, religiously, and culturally diverse people. Since its independence in 1956, Sudan has struggled unsuccessfully to reconcile its ethnic and religious diversity while trying to keep up with the world economy. Civil strife between the North and the South was inevitable when imbalances in political equity, economic development, and social representation became unbridgeable. The mismanagement of Sudan has led to armed conflicts, humanitarian crises, the degradation of natural resources, and chronic poverty.

Today Sudan enters a new era after emerging from more than two decades of war. The North has set up a new power-sharing administration with the South and turned around a struggling economy by introducing sound policies. However, Sudan still faces formidable economic problems and has yet another humanitarian crisis on its hands. Sustainable progress will be difficult until the opposing sides can live peacefully together. Until Sudan's differences are reconciled, this vast country and its friendly, hospitable people will suffer the pain and hardships of war and famine.

GEOGRAPHY

SUDAN IS THE LARGEST COUNTRY IN AFRICA, around one-third of the size of the United States with a land area of nearly 1 million square miles (2.6 million km). Aside from the main urban areas, it is sparsely populated, with an estimated population of about 41 million people. It is bordered by Egypt, Libya, Chad, the Central African Republic, Zaire, Uganda, Kenya, Ethiopia, and Eritrea, and part of its northeastern maritime border lies along the Red Sea.

Sudan can be divided into four distinct geographical regions. In the north is desert, covering about 30 percent of the country's total land area. South of the desert is semiarid grassland and low hills covering most of central Sudan. Farther south is a vast swamp known as the Sudd, while the extreme south is rain forest. There are several low mountain ranges around the borders of the country. The River Nile flows generally from south to north.

Opposite: **Pyramids found in the desert near Atbara, site of the ancient Meroë civilization.**

Below: **The Nile River near Sesebi provides the village with water for irrigation, household use, and transportation.**

A steamer on the White Nile transporting people and goods.

THE NILE

Giving Sudan its very existence, the Nile is the most important feature of life in the country. Its waters, which can give life to the land, can also be destructive. The Nile is the longest river in the world: its most remote headstream is in Burundi, in central Africa, and from that point until it enters the Mediterranean Sea the river is 4,145 miles (6,670 km) long.

The Nile enters Sudan at Nimule on the border with Uganda, and it later becomes known as the White Nile. It flows sluggishly for about 100 miles (161 km) through tropical jungle to Juba, a frontier-style town, and continues north to Gondokoro, where the river gains speed, passing over a series of unnavigable rapids. From there it flows into the Sudd, a vast swamp, and becomes a series of changing channels through thick beds of reeds and mud banks. North of the Sudd the river is joined by the Bahr al-Ghazal and Sobat rivers.

The Blue Nile is a much more turbulent river. It has its origins in Lake Tana, a crater lake in the highlands of Ethiopia. It enters Sudan through a gorge that is almost a mile (1.5 km) deep in places. This gorge was not fully mapped until the 1960s, because it is so difficult to access. The river crosses the flat hot plains of eastern Sudan to join the White Nile at Khartoum. The reason the Nile never dries up is because the Blue Nile carries far more water than the White Nile. It provides most of the Middle Nile's water through the long, hot summers and irrigates about 70 percent of the irrigated land in Sudan.

Two hundred miles (322 km) north of Khartoum the Nile meets the Atbara River, a minor tributary. The Atbara flows for less than half of the year, during the rainy season from June to September. When the Nile floods it carries with it much of the rich black soil that once made the Nile Delta, in Egypt, so fertile. Since the Aswan Dam was built in Egypt, this rich silt no longer reaches the delta but builds up under water in Lake Nasser.

THE MIDDLE NILE

The Middle Nile is a distinct geographical region that extends from the meeting of the Blue Nile and the White Nile at Khartoum to the First Cataract at Aswan in Egypt. In this region, it is demarcated geographically by several cataracts (series of rapids).

The lifeblood of the region is the river itself; it is used for irrigation—water is pumped or dammed into irrigation systems—and deposits fertile soil in the Nile floodplain, which is cultivated in the drier seasons. Irrigation along the banks of the river creates a narrow strip of vegetation quite different from that of the surrounding area. In some places the strip is only 109 yards (100 m) wide; in others it is nonexistent—the desert comes

Within the desert are oases, small pockets of land that support a tiny amount of life, and deep wells. El Obeid is a large oasis town whose water supply often dries up completely, making it dependent on trucked-in water.

right to the edge of the river. As a result of desert sandstorms there is a buildup of sand on some of the west bank of the river. This shifting sand continually encroaches on irrigated fields and settlements.

On either side of this fertile, cultivated strip is a vast area of savanna (semiarid grassland) where the inhabitants are nomadic herders who travel around the area to find grazing land for their animals. Because drought and the encroaching desert have reduced the area of grassland, the herders have experienced serious hardship, loss of animals, and starvation.

Desert lies just beyond this strip of fertile, irrigated land.

CONTROLLING THE RIVER

The English first built a dam at Aswan in 1899; its height was raised in 1912 and in 1933. A second, higher dam was built in the 1960s, which affected the lives of some 50,000 Sudanese. As the waters rose, 27 villages and the town of Wadi Halfa were submerged. The people were compensated and relocated at Khasm el Girba, east of Khartoum. Lake Nasser, also known as Lake Nubia in Sudan, created by the dam, is one of the world's largest reservoirs. Under an international agreement the country of Sudan is allowed to draw 20.5 billion cubic feet (70.8 million cubic meters) of water from Lake Nasser, making major development projects possible.

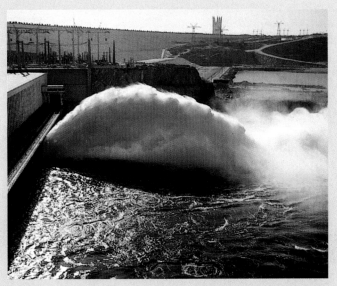

South of Khartoum are the Sennar Dam, built after World War I, and a dam on the White Nile at Jabal Awliya, built in 1937. The Roseires irrigation project, located on the Blue Nile and served by the Roseires Dam, has brought more than 865,511 acres (350,260 ha) of land under cultivation. Another major project, abandoned in the 1980s because of the civil war, was the Jonglei Canal. This canal was intended to divert some of the water of the White Nile where it makes a large bend north of Juba. Environmentalists believed that the canal would have caused a large area of the Sudd to dry up, killing the wildlife in the area.

DESERT

About 30 percent of Sudan's land area is desert. To the west is the Libyan Desert, which has supplied vast amounts of oil farther west in Libya. The Nubian Desert is a region in northeast Sudan. The bits of fertile land along the Nile are known locally as Batn el Hagar, or "the belly of stones."

Sudan is undergoing a period of rapid desertification because of global climate change and the harsh demands being made on the savanna. Plants are unable to survive drought, the harvesting of firewood, and grazing by animals.

MOUNTAINS

There are four major mountainous areas in Sudan.

The Red Sea Hills, in the northeast, are low-lying stony hills near the coast. The terrain here is like that of the rest of northern Sudan.

The Jebel Marra, mountains in the west, are distinctive, rounded pillars of rock that stand out over the lower wooded slopes. The mountain valleys have rich, fertile soil, making the region agriculturally productive. The highest point of the range is an extinct volcano called Gimbala at 10,075 feet (3,071 m). It has hot springs, waterfalls, and mountain pools. Inside the crater itself is a lake colored green by sulphur.

In the center of the country are the Nuba Mountains, and to the south are the Immatong and Dingotona ranges. Sudan's highest peak is Mount Kinyeti at 10,460 feet (3,187 m), close to the border with Uganda.

The Red Sea Hills.

CLIMATE

Sudan is one of Africa's hottest countries. The northern third of the country, the Nubian and Libyan deserts, are dry all year. They experience occasional flash thunderstorms that last just a few minutes and that, in some areas, may occur only once in a generation. Temperatures range from 100°F to 113°F (38°C–45°C) between May and September but can fall to almost 32°F (0°C) between November and March. Wind blows continually from the north, often whipping up sandstorms known as *haboobs* (ha-BOOBS), which last for a short time, darkening the sky and bringing gale-force winds. They are rarely accompanied by rain.

A schoolteacher walks on desert sand dunes that have engulfed an entire village.

The middle and southern thirds of the country experience a hot and wet season and a hot and dry season. The southwest experiences the highest rainfall. The rainy season starts in April and lasts until November; it provides as much as 60 inches (152 cm) of rain per year. As one travels north the rainy season grows shorter. Khartoum, at the very edge of the desert, has the least rain—on average about 4 inches (10 cm) between July and August. Temperatures are highest just before the rainy season and lowest during December and January. In Khartoum the average temperature is 89°F (32°C) in July and 74°F (23°C) in December.

The Red Sea area has a humid climate determined by its position on the coast. It has two rainy seasons, one in the winter and the other corresponding to the summer rainy season of the Middle Nile.

THE SUDD

The Sudd, meaning "barrier" in Arabic, is a swamp covering about 9,000 square miles (23,310 square km), larger than the state of New Hampshire in the United States and roughly the size of Wales in the United Kingdom.

For thousands of years it stood as a physical barrier between the North and the South of Sudan, halting the earliest recorded search for the source of the Nile, sent by the ancient Egyptians, Greeks, and Roman emperor Nero in A.D. 60, and every other search until the 19th century. In the early 20th century the British cut a permanent waterway through the Sudd. It is still navigable today. The few travelers who make the journey see mile after mile of swamp, dominated by papyrus plants.

The Jonglei Canal project, now abandoned, would have destroyed the Sudd, because the water that feeds it would have been channeled into irrigation projects to the north. The Sudd is one of the few remaining areas of its kind in the world, and its destruction would have decimated many species that depend on it. The halting of the canal project has given the Sudd a reprieve, but at the same time farming projects that might have provided food and prevented starvation are suspended. However, plans to restart the digging of the Jonglei Canal have surfaced and so have fears that the draining of the Sudd would cause irreparable damage.

PAPYRUS

The papyrus plant flourishes in the Sudd, dominating the landscape and helping to create a surface solid enough for animals to walk across. It is a member of the sedge family and needs very moist, swamplike conditions to survive. It grows to about 10 feet (3 m) in height and has long woody roots that have a strong perfume and spread under the surface of the water, anchoring the tall plant.

The papyrus formed an important part of the ancient civilizations of Sudan and Egypt. Its roots were dried and used for fuel, while the pith in the stem was, and still is, boiled and eaten. The pith was also the raw material from which paper was made. It was sliced into strips and laid out lengthwise, and other layers were put over it crosswise. The whole fabric was moistened, pressed, dried, and rubbed smooth. It was made into scrolls of paper 20 feet (6 m) in length.

Besides paper, papyrus was used to make boxes, sandals, and even boats. A man named Thor Heyerdahl built a boat of papyrus in 1970 and sailed it from North Africa to the West Indies.

Elephants still live in the wildlife parks of southern Sudan.

Tamarisk trees exude an edible honeylike substance called manna, thought to be the manna eaten by the Israelites in their flight from Egypt.

FAUNA

Sudan has an enormous variety of wildlife, the result of its varied habitats—from the desert to the swampy Sudd to the rain forests of the South.

In the South animals such as zebras, lions, leopards, gazelles, antelopes, and many kinds of primates still survive in the wild. Crocodiles and hippopotamuses can be seen in the Nile.

There are herds of wild elephants in what remains of wildlife parks such as Nimule in southern Sudan. The shortage of ivory caused by world bans has brought about a lucrative industry in Sudan. Poachers have taken advantage of the war to kill elephants for their ivory, and there has been a direct trade of ivory for weapons between the southern fighters and whomever they can get weapons from. It is thought that between 6,000 and 12,000 elephants a year have died as a result.

The wildlife in the Nuba Mountains has also suffered. As part of a scorched-earth policy in the war against the Nuba, most of the animals that might have been hunted for food have been destroyed.

FLORA

The flora of the region varies as widely as does its animal life. In the South is rain forest, areas where huge buttressed trees block out the sunlight and smaller shade-loving plants survive beneath. North of the papyrus swamps of the Sudd, the plant life becomes more and more dependent on the river for its survival, forming a thin strip of vegetation along the river banks.

In the Middle Nile are large areas of savanna, sandy soil covered by tall grasses and low drought-resistant trees. The seasonal rains bring a sudden burst of life to the plants here. Of all the land in Sudan, the savanna is under the most intense pressure from drought, the cutting of firewood, and overgrazing.

Farther north little plant life grows except during occasional rain showers that allow dormant seeds to quickly germinate, flower, and produce new seeds, which then lie dormant, waiting for the next rain.

An interesting plant that grows in the South and the Middle Nile is the baobab tree. Its huge trunk can grow to a diameter of 30 feet (9 m). It produces an edible fruit that is made into a cooling drink. The bark is harvested for rope-making.

Another plant with a multiplicity of uses is the date palm, which can be seen all along the banks of the Nile and in the oases. Besides its edible fruit, its leaves, fibers, trunk, and sap are used to make baskets, mats, crates, furniture, sawdust, brooms, rope, roof beams, footbridges, and wine.

A man climbs up a date palm. The date palm is valuable in Sudan as almost every part of the plant can be used.

17

MAJOR TOWNS

The capital city of Sudan is Khartoum; together with its neighboring cities of Omdurman and Khartoum North and their suburbs, they form a bustling metropolis with a population of about 6 million. These cities, at the confluence of the two Niles, form the industrial, commercial, and communications center of Sudan.

The British laid out Khartoum's gardens and tree-lined avenues, and many of the old colonial buildings built by the British are still in use, although they are rather shabby now. Beside these, more modern multistory buildings have sprung up. Omdurman and other parts of Khartoum are more Arab in style, with flat-roofed single-story houses, narrow alleyways, beautiful mosques, and of course the souk, the city market. Five bridges and outboard motorboats carry passengers and their goods between Khartoum, Omdurman, and Khartoum North. In the years of drought and war many refugees from southern Sudan, Darfur, and neighboring countries came to Khartoum to live in poorly built shantytowns around the city's edge.

Another large city in Sudan is Port Sudan, on the east coast. It was built to accommodate the trade across the Red Sea and to other coastal countries. Today Port Sudan is the main export center for cotton, peanuts, and oil. An international airport and an oil refinery are located in proximity to the city.

Wadi Halfa, near the Egyptian border, survives on the trade between Egypt and Sudan. A considerable black market exists for scarce goods

Khartoum, the capital of Sudan, has a mixture of Arabic, colonial, and modern buildings.

in this region. Buildings are traditional one-story flat-roofed structures, often enclosing a central courtyard with trees to create some shade in the searing heat of the afternoons.

The major town of the South is Juba, a trading post on the last navigable point of the Nile before the border with Uganda. The British traders and missionaries who constructed the town built cathedrals, large bungalows with gardens, and wide boulevards shaded by trees. The buildings are still there, although affected by heavy use and the climate. Like Port Sudan and Khartoum, Juba has large shantytowns set up by nomadic herders displaced by the war. Various aid groups are stationed in Juba from time to time, with many returning since the end of the fighting. More flights have traveled to Juba's small airport since the war was concluded in 2005.

Port Sudan is the country's major trading port on the Red Sea.

HISTORY

SUDAN IS A COUNTRY WITH several very distinct ethnic and geographical areas. Its history from the earliest times reflects those divisions. The northern and middle areas of Sudan, north of Khartoum, have a fairly well recorded history linked with the Egyptian and Nubian empires. The known history of the southern area covers a much shorter period of only a few hundred years, with archaeology filling in the gaps.

THE MIDDLE NILE

The area of modern Sudan known as the Middle Nile, from Khartoum in the South to Aswan in the North, has had a special part to play in the history of the world. The earliest cities in Africa south of Egypt, built by the Kushite or Kerma civilization, developed along this stretch of the Nile. North of the Middle Nile is the Middle East and Arab culture; south lies the barrier of the Sudd, surrounded by "black" Africa. Historically the Nile was a major route into Africa where ivory, gold, and slaves could be bought or taken. The area remained a major trade route until

Opposite: **The Mahdi's tomb in Khartoum.**

TRAVELERS FROM KUSH

One of the outstanding features of the people of Kush, who built the earliest cities in Africa south of Egypt, was their love of travel and new ideas.

They traded with the Egyptians in the north, and hints of their presence have been found as far west as Lake Chad. Through their ports on the Red Sea they traded with Arabia, East Africa, India, and perhaps even China. Wherever they went they brought back new things and new ideas. A Roman bronze head made in Alexandria has been found in the ruins of ancient Meroë, and Greek and Roman influence can be seen in the temple architecture.

Evidence has also been found of Kushite ambassadors in Rome, and a servant of the queen of Meroë is believed to have met the apostle Philip on the road from Jerusalem to Gaza.

the development of camel routes across the Sahara in the first millennium A.D., followed in the 16th century by sailing ships trading along the coasts of Africa.

ANCIENT HISTORY

The earliest structures discovered in Sudan are in the region of the Third Cataract, separate from the modern Egyptian border. They are a series of palaces, temples, and residences built in the third millennium B.C. by the ancient Nubians at Kerma.

The oldest city of the Kush civilization, Kerma was situated at the Third Cataract between about 2500 and 1500 B.C. in a period when Egyptian influence was low. The small city was established in one of the rare areas where river water could be channeled easily to low-lying land. It is the earliest known non-Egyptian African city. It had a complex social structure and rulers who were buried with large numbers of human sacrifices—the most ever found in burials anywhere in the world. The settlement included a huge cemetery, buildings used for storage and religious activities, a lightly fortified city, and craft centers. It is thought that the town was a transport and assembly point for exports from the southern Middle Nile into Egypt.

Around 1500 B.C. the Egyptian empire's conquest in the Middle Nile extended almost as far as the Fifth Cataract. Fortified towns were gradually replaced by less-military settlements with temples dedicated to the Egyptian gods. This second wave of Egyptian influence in Kush ended around 1000 B.C., mainly because of political problems in Egypt itself, and possibly because of low water levels in the Nile, which would have made trade difficult.

Egyptian influence can be seen in this stone statue in the National Museum in Khartoum.

NAPATA AND MEROË

Around the ninth century B.C., Kushite civilization was reborn with the Napata kingdom, which has left behind the ruins of temples, cemeteries, and towns. At one time, around the eighth and seventh centuries B.C, this kingdom was so powerful it controlled the whole of Egypt. Napata's rulers were also called pharaohs and copied Egyptian customs; decorations in temple ruins show Egyptian gods with curly hair and African features. The society used Egyptian hieroglyphics, as is evident from tomb and temple inscriptions.

The kingdom of Meroë came into existence around 400 B.C., as Napata declined, and lasted nearly 700 years. The ruins of Meroë reveal a palace with baths and plumbing, factories, houses, and evidence of an iron-smelting works. It was a civilization based on farming the banks of the Nile, which were lined with farms and small towns. Small pyramidal tombs held the bodies of kings and queens, and the Lion Temple has exterior paintings showing the rulers of Meroë with the Lion God.

Meroë existed concurrently with the Greek and Roman domination of Egypt. It was attacked by the Roman Empire in 23 B.C., suffered repeated attacks by nomadic groups in the following centuries, and was finally conquered by the Axumite empire of Ethiopia in about A.D. 350.

It was during the Meroë era that the ox-drawn water-wheel came into use, enabling large, previously uninhabited areas of the Middle Nile to be irrigated and settled.

23

SELUKA, SHADOOF, AND SAQUIA

The human settlement of the Middle Nile region depended on the river. In one season the Nile could destroy crops and houses by flooding; the next it could be so low that the fields could not be irrigated and crops died. In one year it might bring rich soil up from the South to grow the next season's crops, while in another year it might wash all the arable soil away. There was also the problem of getting water to the arable land. Three types of land existed, each defined by the type of irrigation system it required.

Seluka land was situated on the floodplain of the river. Each year soil and water were carried up by the river, and all the farmer had to do was plant his crops, weed them, and watch them grow. The drawback of this land was that it could be cultivated only during one season.

Shadoof land was the next to develop. It was the land that lay 10 feet (3 m) or less above the river, so that water could be lifted up to it using a man-powered pivot.

Saquia land was around 25 feet (8 m) above the level of the river and came into cultivation only after the invention of the ox-drawn waterwheel.

A fourth type of land, rare in the Sudan, was basin land, which lay adjacent to the river but at a lower level. River water could be channeled into it by means of a canal or when the river overflowed.

CHRISTIANITY

By about the sixth century A.D., what is now northern Sudan was settled by three major kingdoms, all of which practiced Christianity. Christianity had spread through the Roman Empire into Egypt and, later, to Sudan and Ethiopia.

The Nubian Christian kingdoms built beautiful churches and extensive cities; the ruins of these cities are still being discovered. Elite houses in the cities had plumbing, indoor toilets, and frescoes on the walls, and the residents drank from imported glassware.

ISLAM

Gradually this sophisticated urban lifestyle gave way to a Muslim sultanate dominated by Arabs who brought their own religion—Islam. The largest of the sultanates was the Funj kingdom of Sennar, which survived into the early 19th century. The Funj sultan's wealth came from slaves and gold mines close to the border with modern Ethiopia.

At the start of the 19th century the Arab sheikhdoms of Sudan were attacked by the forces of the ruler of Egypt, Muhammad Ali. He had seized power in Egypt with the use of a Turkish slave army that he sent south with one of his sons to take slaves and gold. The troops ventured into and beyond the Sudd. They sent back 30,000 slaves and the ears of those they killed. During the return journey one of Ali's sons was killed, and in retribution Ali sent more troops and took control of Sudan. Egyptian rule lasted 63 years.

The ruins of Christian churches are still being discovered beneath the desert sands.

A 17th-century French doctor visited the Funj kingdom and described the sultan's enormous wealth and power.

The son of a
boatbuilder, the
Mahdi claimed
that he was chosen
by God to be a
representative
of the Prophet
Muhammad.

SLAVERY

The Christian Nubian kingdom of Pongola negotiated a pact with Egypt in A.D. 652 for an annual tribute of slaves to Egyptians. The Muslims formalized this slave-taking by arranging treaties with the Nubians to exchange slaves for Egyptian goods. Slavery became a tradition that lasted for thousands of years and dominated North-South relations. Until the gradual suppression of slavery in the 1860s, the slave trade was the most profitable undertaking in Sudan. It was also the focus of Egyptian interest in the country. A form of slavery has been revived in modern times, with southern Sudanese being forced into local militias and domestic service in the North.

COLONIALISM AND THE MAHDI

The reconstruction of the Suez Canal in the 19th century attracted both British and French attention. The French were keen on assisting in the reconstruction and established the Suez Canal Company in 1858. The construction of the canal used tens of thousands of people in forced labor. Meanwhile the British viewed the French project as a threat to their geopolitical and financial interest. When Egypt not only went heavily into debt over the building of the Suez Canal but also failed to establish effective control over southern Sudan, it gave Britain the opportunity to intervene in the region. Forced labor was condemned, and the project was stopped. In 1877 General Charles Gordon was appointed governor of Sudan and Egypt.

While the Turco–Egyptians and the British were establishing their authority, a local leader emerged. Muhammad Ahmad declared himself a Mahdi, or savior, elected by God to lead a jihad, or holy war. He called for Sudan to be ruled according to the laws of Islam. The Mahdi took the towns of Kordofan and Darfur by siege, killing the European and Turkish leaders, and starving out the troops. Hearing of the unrest, the British sent General Gordon to Khartoum to hold the city against the Mahdi. Gordon asked for reinforcements too late; the city was taken and Gordon killed. His head was put on a pole to taunt the relieving troops.

The Mahdists held power for 13 years while Britain and other colonial powers conquered other regions of Africa, dividing up the land to be exploited. Eventually a campaign against the Mahdists was organized. General Herbert Kitchener was sent with troops from Egypt, arriving in Omdurman on September 2, 1898. They were attacked by 60,000 Mahdists armed with swords and shields and wearing suits of armor. Eleven thousand Sudanese died, and the British gained power in Sudan.

The Mahdi.

INDEPENDENCE

The Anglo–Egyptian condominium remained in joint control of Sudan until World War II. In 1946 Britain and Egypt began negotiations to decide Sudan's future, but they ended in deadlock, as Egypt demanded British withdrawal, and Britain wanted to remain in control.

In 1948 the British began a process of giving Sudan the choice of union with Egypt or independence. They established a legislature, which the pro-Egyptians boycotted, and in December 1950 the legislature passed a motion asking Britain and Egypt for independence.

Meanwhile, the Egyptian National Assembly named King Farouk of Egypt the sole ruler of Sudan, but after his abdication in 1952 Egypt and Britain agreed to grant independence to Sudan. In 1953 the first elections were held, and a three-year period of replacing British and Egyptian officials with Sudanese began.

CIVIL WAR

At this stage the enormous social and political differences between the North and the South began to make themselves felt even more acutely.

During the British administration the two halves of the country had been kept separate, but with the new pro-Egyptian party in power, southern elements began to see a threat to their control over their own affairs. In August 1955 a mutiny among southern regiments broke out.

Sudan formally became a republic on January 1, 1956. Elections were held in February 1958, and the Umma Party, led by Abdallah Khalil, came to power. His government was formed from a coalition of small parties and was quite unstable. Within six months interparty quarrels and national strikes ended the government.

Power was seized by General Ibrahim Abbud, the chief of staff of the armed forces. He outlawed strikes and political parties, and under his military government, which remained in power for six years, Sudan's economy began to improve.

A low-key rebellion continued in the South. Finally there was an unarmed mass rebellion against the military rulers, and they agreed to step down. Elections followed, and in May 1965 parliamentary rule was reestablished.

AL-NIMEIRY

In 1969 a second military coup brought Colonel Jaafar al-Nimeiry to power. Political parties were again banned, and a degree of economic stability returned. This military government withstood 22 attempted coups before the 23rd one succeeded. One of the most optimistic aspects of al-Nimeiry's rule was the peace accord he made with the southern forces at Addis Ababa in 1972, which gave the South a large amount of regional autonomy and halted the war.

Al-Nimeiry began a series of projects to make Sudan a major food supplier, including the Jonglei Canal project. But his loans from the

Sudan became a member of the Arab League in January 1956 and a member of the United Nations in November of the same year.

International Monetary Fund caused dissent when he was forced to raise food prices to meet debt repayments.

To gain support wherever he could, al-Nimeiry turned to the conservative northern Islamic groups, declaring shariah law in 1983. This meant that throughout the country every citizen, regardless of religion, was bound by the laws of Islam.

Angered by the imposition of Islamic laws, the non-Muslim people in the South took up arms once more. They were led this time by John Garang, a U.S. economics graduate, who formed the Sudan People's Liberation Army (SPLA). The northerners quickly lost control of the South. A state of emergency was declared, and the revolt expanded.

In 1985 there was a successful election, and Sayyid Sadiq al-Mahdi, great-grandson of the Mahdi, became the new leader of Sudan.

Southern villages lie deserted after raids by both government and rebel troops. Their occupants fled to refugee camps and shantytowns.

Islamic law forbids the consumption of alcohol. When al-Nimeiry declared shariah law, the entire Sudanese stock of alcohol was poured into the Nile.

AL-BASHIR

For the next four years there was a return to civilian parliamentary government and a purge of Islamic extremists. But shariah law continued, and food shortages and economic decline were made worse by the war and drought in the South. Another military coup took place in 1989, led by Brigadier Omar Hassan al-Bashir. He declared a state of emergency, political opposition was again suppressed, and the war against the South was stepped up. Moves toward democracy began again in 1993, and by 2002 al-Bashir had brokered a ceasefire with the SPLA with the Machakos Protocol, a statement of intent to end the war. Although there were disputes over sharing power, by 2003 hostilities were formally declared over, with al-Bashir remaining as president and Garang as vice president. The peace deal was signed and finalized in Nairobi, giving regional autonomy to the South and ending more than 22 years of civil war.

DARFUR CONFLICT

Unfortunately the peace process was overshadowed by armed rebellion in Darfur in the west. Having felt long ignored in the peace process, two new rebel groups, the Sudan Liberation Army (SLA) and the Justice and Equality Movement, attacked in 2003 seeking greater autonomy for the Fur, Masalit, and Zaghawa tribes. The government responded by arming Arab militias, the Janjaweed (JOHN-ja-weed), to put down the insurrection. More than 200,000 Arab and non-Arab people in the region were killed, and more than 2 million people fled from their homes. In May 2006 the SLA signed a peace agreement with the government, but the other rebel group rejected the offer. As of 2006 the situation had yet to stabilize. Currently the African Union has stationed 7,000 troops to monitor human-rights abuses and protect civilians.

John Garang died in a helicopter crash a few months after the signing of the 2003 peace treaty. He was succeeded by Salva Kiir.

CHAD–SUDAN CONFLICT

The Darfur conflict spilled over to neighboring Chad when Janjaweed militias and Chadian rebel groups, allegedly aided by the Sudanese government, raided villages in Abeché, in eastern Chad, in pursuit of 200,000 asylum-seeking Fur refugees. The raid displaced more than 30,000 Chadian villagers and killed several others. In 2006 the Tripoli Agreement was signed to bring ceasefire to the conflict, but rebel activities continued. The recent attack on N'Djamena has led Chad to close its borders and break off all diplomatic relations with Sudan.

President al-Bashir reviews his troops at his government's inauguration.

GOVERNMENT

SUDAN HAS EXPERIENCED MANY FORMS of government over the centuries: small city-states ruled by a king or a queen, rule by foreign powers, parliamentary democracy, military juntas. In modern times it has been a politically and socially diverse country with many small factional groups vying for control. Successive governments have had to form coalitions with powerful interest groups to maintain power. One of the most powerful groups of all has been the northern Islamic organization. The brief spell of peace between the North and the South ended when the southern groups saw the adoption of shariah law in 1983 as a dismissal of the peace they had made in 1972. Sudan has subsequently experienced full-scale civil war between government troops and the SPLA. In January 2005 the government of Sudan signed a peace deal, the Comprehensive

Left: **Marchers carry pictures of John Garang and former president Jaafar al-Nimeiry in a political rally.**

Opposite: **The government building in Khartoum.**

Politicians at a pre-election conference in Port Sudan.

Peace Agreement (CPA), to end warring with the South. A six-year interim period was agreed upon, followed by a referendum on self-determination for the South. The terms of the CPA allowed the government to share its administrative powers and oil revenues with the SPLA and to grant varying degrees of autonomy to disputed areas in the South.

THE STRUCTURE OF GOVERNMENT

Sudan is officially a presidential republic, where all effective political power is in the hands of the president. In the past decade it has been a one-party presidential republic, a military regime, a parliamentary democracy, another military regime, and a transitional state between military rule and parliamentary democracy.

Currently, the Government of National Unity, made up of the majority partner, the National Congress Party, and the SPLA, make up a power-sharing government, as agreed under the CPA. Omar Hassan al-Bashir remains president, with the head of the SPLA—John Garang, followed by Salva Kiir—as first vice president and Ali Taha as vice president. Kiir also heads the interim administration in the South.

THE PRESIDENCY

The president theoretically holds office for six years, although coup attempts often interrupt this process. After the 1985 coup, when Sudan spent a brief time as a democracy, there was no president. Instead the role was carried out by a five-man Supreme Council.

THE CONSTITUTION

The new Interim National Constitution and the Constitution of Southern Sudan were ratified and signed in 2005 by Sudan's National Assembly and the legislative council of the SPLA. The national constitution allows for the freedom to form political parties and freedom of speech. It describes the presidency, the legislature, and the judiciary. The constitution is to be in effect for the six-year interim period as stated in the CPA. Any amendments to the constitution need to be approved by at least three-quarters of the National Legislature.

Currently the presidency is held by General al-Bashir, who has kept the post since 1989. He is also the prime minister and the commander in chief of the armed forces. He was "elected" in 1996 when a call was made for a new president and National Assembly. As president, al-Bashir has the power to suspend the constitution and declare a state of emergency, a prerogative that has been used several times by Sudanese presidents. In 1999 al-Bashir did call for a state of emergency and dissolved the National Assembly in the wake of parliament speaker al-Turabi's call for reducing the powers of the president and reestablishing the role of the prime minister. The National Assembly resumed in 2001 after al-Bashir was "reelected" in 2000 for a second term amid boycotts by the opposition and accusations of vote rigging.

THE LEGISLATURE

The National Legislature, formed following the signing of the CPA, is officially bicameral, replacing the 360-seat unicameral National Assembly. The National Legislature is made up of the new version of the National Assembly, consisting of 450 president-appointed members, and the Council States, consisting of 50 members indirectly elected by state legislatures. The Council States are made up of two representatives from each state. All members of the National Legislature serve a six-year term.

Currently Sudan's National Legislature is dominated by al-Bashir's National Congress Party, which holds 52 percent of the seats. The SPLA has 28 percent. Fourteen percent of the seats are given to other northerners and 6 percent to other southerners. Although opposition parties are allowed, they have little chance of gaining power.

Sudan alienated many of its overseas political allies by declaring its support for Iraq in the Gulf War and offering sanctuary to Osama bin Laden. However, Sudan eventually cooperated with the United States and gave access to its files on Iraq and al-Qaeda.

THE JUDICIARY

Islamic laws have not been imposed in the South, but non-Muslims living in the North have been punished under these laws.

The legal system in Sudan is generally based on shariah law. Citizens in the North are subject to shariah law regardless of their religion. However, with the CPA of 2005, southern states are allowed to legislate according to the beliefs and customs of the southerners. They are also permitted to amend national legislation with the approval of the Council States.

There are four levels of courts for civil issues and five for criminal issues. At the bottom of the hierarchy are the Town Benches, followed by the District Court, the Province Courts, and the Courts of Appeal. At the top of the hierarchy is the Supreme Court, which is the final court of appeal.

SHARIAH LAW

Except in the three southern provinces, shariah law is imposed throughout the country. Penalties determined by shariah law apply to all citizens, except in the South, regardless of their own religion. Public lashing is common for those found guilty of drinking alcohol or uttering blasphemy, for which the maximum sentence is 100 lashes. For a theft of anything valued at more than $40, the right hand is amputated. For aggravated theft or more-serious crimes, the right hand and the left foot are amputated.

Adultery and repeated homosexuality are punishable by execution, but in both cases the enormous burden of proof has prevented these punishments from being carried out. Those convicted of "shameful" acts are lashed; this is quite common in cases of suspected adultery. Those found engaging in premarital sex are also lashed, with the guilty receiving the maximum 100 lashes.

Those injured by crime can demand retribution. For example, a woman whose arm was broken can demand that the arm of the woman who caused the injury be broken also.

A Shilluk king and his bodyguards. In isolated areas, especially in the South, federal laws give way to tribal customs and local militia.

All the judges in the judicial system throughout the North are appointed by the president aided by advice from the National Judiciary Service Commission. In the South, however, the president of the Government of Southern Sudan appoints the judges.

MILITARY DEFENSE

The Sudanese People's Armed Forces make up Sudan's military arm. Historically the military forces received inadequate training and had limited and outdated equipment and poor maintenance capabilities. The situation was made worse in the 1990s with the dismissals of professional officer corps. At times the government has had to enlist the assistance of rebel groups and Arab militia to fight insurrections. Today Sudan's military defense is equipped with modern weapons from Libya, China, and Russia. It has 105,000 members, including 20,000 conscripts. The army is the largest unit, followed by the air force and the navy. Together they are charged with the defense of Sudan's external borders and the preservation of internal security.

The Sudanese army is organized into 10 divisions, including one armored, one mechanized, and six infantry divisions. The air force and the navy have an estimated 3,000 and 1,800 personnel respectively. The navy is based at Khartoum, Port Sudan, and Marsa Gwiyai.

LOCAL GOVERNMENT

The organization of local government has been through numerous changes. In the period between 1983 and 1997, the country was divided into eight regions, each headed by a military governor. In 1997 the eight regions were replaced with 26 states. Executives, cabinets, and senior officials to those states are all appointed by the president. The state of Khartoum is administered by a governor. Each state has a small budget as determined by Khartoum, making it economically dependent on the central government.

POLITICAL PARTIES

Political parties in Sudan undergo periods of being banned interspersed with periods of relative freedom. In 1998 the constitution permitted political "associations" provided that they were registered with the government. More than 30 political parties registered, and all democratic governments have been made up of coalitions of these parties.

The most prominent is the ruling party, the National Congress Party. Headed by President al-Bashir and Ibrahim Umar, it is the successor to the former National Islamic Front. The second most influential party is the National Democratic Alliance (NDA), the umbrella group of opposition parties based in Cairo and Eritrea. It is made up of the SPLA, which has formed a coalition with the current government to share political power; the Sudan People's Liberation Movement (SPLM), the political wing of the SPLA; the Beja Congress; and the Democratic Unionist Party (DUP), which is a centrist/right-wing Muslim group.

The main political pressure group is the Popular Arab-Islamic Conference, which is involved in the Darfur insurgency. It is headed by Hassan al-Turabi, who supports a hard-line Islamist regime.

HUMAN RIGHTS

An SPLA officer and his troops.

Sudan has a record of human-rights abuses by both government and rebel forces. The government has placed restrictions on freedoms of assembly, speech, religious practice, and political association. The media and the judicial system are thus tightly controlled and subjected to government interference. Government security forces are also said to operate "ghost houses," secret detention centers where political opponents are taken for harsh interrogation. Amnesty International has recorded many cases of illegal detention and torture of political opponents of the government.

Amnesty International also blames both government and rebel forces for the "disappearance" of thousands of civilians in the South and the Nuba Mountains. More recently in Darfur, the government and rebel forces have committed atrocities, murdering, raping, and driving millions of people from their homes into refugee camps. The delivery of humanitarian aid to the area is also restricted. In the North, the age-old practice of enslaving southern boys as young as 12 years old persists.

ECONOMY

SUDAN'S ECONOMY has made vast improvements since the 1960s, when the country saw zero economic growth. By 1996 inflation was running at 130 percent. In the late 1990s Sudan started implementing the International Monetary Fund (IMF) macroeconomic reforms in a bid to revive its economic outlook. Sudan has also begun exporting crude oil. The increased oil production, coupled with improvements in monetary policies and infrastructure investment, improved Sudan's economy. Oil production alone makes up an estimated 80 percent of Sudan's export earnings. Agricultural production remains an important sector, employing 80 percent of Sudan's work force. In 2004 Sudan sustained growth of its gross domestic product (GDP), the total annual value of goods and services produced by a nation, at 8.6 percent.

Above: **An artisan at work in Omdurman.**

Opposite: **With a large number of Sudanese rearing livestock for a living, a natural by-product, leather, is fully utilized to make footwear.**

However, the current rebellion in Darfur, corruption, huge international debts, famine, drought, the influx of foreign refugees, and weak world agricultural prices have brought about a near-impossible economic situation. Although many foreign countries were willing to invest in exploration and development projects, Sudan's chronic political instability has brought many of the major development projects in the South to a standstill. Sudan also has numerous undeveloped and neglected infrastructures. One example is the expensive Jonglei Canal project. Due in part to the long-standing war between the Muslim North and the Christian South, the project was abandoned and destroyed although it was near completion.

Sudan's inflation rate reached 133 percent in 1996. Since then it has fallen to a much lower 9 percent in 2005.

All the above factors ensured that Sudan remains one of the poorest and least developed countries in the world, with much of the population living below the poverty line.

AGRICULTURE

Sudan has the potential to become a major producer of cash crops but suffers, like other cash-crop producers, from the ups and downs of world prices. Sudan has a total land area of more than 618 million acres (250 million ha). About 50 percent of that is potentially prime agricultural land, but only about 17 million acres (6.9 million ha) are actually cultivated. Agriculture is the main source of livelihood for 80 percent of the population. Cotton provides the second-largest export earnings, after the production of oil.

The area south of Khartoum is a major cotton-growing area. Cotton is an important crop for Sudan, accounting for 40-50 percent of exports. It grows well in the hot dry climate around Khartoum but needs constant irrigation. It is harvested largely by hand, then separated from the seed cases in the local cotton-ginning plants. Recently Sudan has been cultivating

GUM ARABIC

Another successful crop is gum arabic, which is used as a thickening agent in cooking and when making candy, adhesives, and drugs. It is also a major ingredient in gelatin capsules. Sudan produces four-fifths of the world supply of gum arabic. It is secreted by a species of acacia tree that grows wild in western Sudan. The walnut-size balls of rubbery matter are harvested in the dry season. Gum arabic is marketed through a company of which the state owns 30 percent. Although the export earnings for gum arabic have been declining since the mid-1990s, it is still a lucrative crop for Sudan.

A harvest of *ful* beans is tossed in the air so that leaves and chaff are blown away by the wind.

a variety of extrafine cotton that is highly resistant to diseases. The cotton industry was nationalized in 1970, and cotton is sold and exported through the Cotton Marketing Board.

Sorghum is another very successful crop in Sudan. It is a drought-resistant grain and has been the staple food of most of Africa for centuries. Besides being an important food crop for the country, it is also an export crop. The sorghum plant grows about 13 feet (4 m) tall and bears a large flower head on which round seeds form. The seeds are ground into flour and made into porridge and flat bread; both are staple foods in Sudan. Sorghum can also be brewed into beer. Another important grain for the local market is rice.

Sesame is also a growing export industry. Other crops include sugarcane, peanuts, onions, and sunflower seeds. Attempts to grow tropical crops such as tobacco, coffee, and tea in the South have been hindered by the war.

THE EL GEZIRA AND RAHAD DEVELOPMENT PROJECTS

The El Gezira project, located between the Blue Nile and the White Nile, was a colonial government development project using industrial farming techniques. Divided into large plots and rented out to cooperative groups, the area produces 48 percent of the country's sorghum, 40-50 percent of its cotton, 22 percent of its millet, and 8 percent of its groundnuts. Although the area is a major producer of cotton, in recent years cotton has steadily been replaced by the growing popularity of sesame and sugarcane.

A similar project is being carried out at Rahad, where land is irrigated using water reserves from the Roseires Dam. The expensive project was financed by the World Bank, the United States, and Kuwait. The land is rented out to tenant farmers, and the proportion of land given to each of several crops is determined by the government. About half of the land produces cotton, while the other half is planted with peanuts and vegetables, producing food for the local market as well as export crops.

The people who farm the land had been there before the project began, but now they must grow crops in the proportion determined by the government. The program has failed for this very reason. As world prices fluctuate farmers should be able to switch crops, but their agreements force them to grow crops that are not in demand. A black economy has developed where farmers secretly grow higher proportions of sorghum, which they can sell locally. They devote the fertilizer given to them to the sorghum and leave the cotton unfertilized, which results in a poor cotton crop.

Sudanese camel traders herd their animals just as cattle drovers once herded cattle across the American plains. Sudan has the longest driving track in the world.

LIVESTOCK

In vast areas of eastern and western Sudan nomads roam with their herds, moving from one oasis to another, cropping the land as they go. The animals are mostly cattle, camels, sheep, and goats.

More than any other section of the economy, the tending of livestock has suffered from the years of drought, famine, and war. The drought brought the herders to the cities to find water, and thousands of the animals died in the long journeys. As animals died the people who depended on them set up shantytowns around the cities or came to depend more and more on refugee camps. In the South, where there was no drought, animals have been taken by raiding troops from both sides of the war and even killed as part of a scorched-earth policy, to stop southern soldiers from finding food. Now that the war in the South is over, livestock production has proved its vast potential by becoming an important contributor to the agricultural economy. Products such as skins and hides have increased livestock proceeds from $97.68 million in 2003 to $137.64 million in 2004.

FORESTRY AND FISHING

Sudan has 165 million acres (67 million ha) of forest area, which is entirely owned by the government. Between 1990 and 2005, 21.8 million acres (8.8 million ha), or about 13 percent, of the forest was logged for firewood. Other forestry products include beeswax, tannin, senna, charcoal, and luxury woods such as mahogany.

Fishing on the Nile is an important local industry, but the fisheries are barely exploited. Nile perch are readily caught from the banks and provide daily food and most of the protein for people living along the river. Dried fish are traded with nomads for milk and other animal products. A fishing industry has also been encouraged along the Red Sea coast.

A nomad girl takes camels to be watered in Darfur.

TRANSPORTATION

Sudan has 12,428–15,535 miles (20,000–25,000 km) of roads but only 2,175 miles (3,500 km) of paved roads. Most people travel on the back of open trucks; often 60 people are crushed into a space in which 20 people would be cramped. Trucks travel across packed-earth tracks that become swamps when it rains and extremely rough when it is dry. Many roads are impassable in the wet season. The roads in Sudan continue to undergo expansion, especially in the North, between Khartoum and the Red Sea. However, most rural areas of the country remain inaccessible by wheeled transport.

Sudan has about 2,486 miles (4,000 km) of navigable waterways on the Nile and its tributaries, although only 1,056 miles (1,700 km) are navigable year-round. The only long-distance passenger ferry in northern Sudan comes weekly, traveling between Wadi Halfa and Aswan. South of Khartoum, the Nile is navigable only as far as Juba.

The national air carrier, Sudan Airways, holds a monopoly on domestic flights. Currently the company is being privatized, which people hope will do away with the lack of trained personnel and the scheduling and maintenance problems. Sudan has approximately 88 airports, but only 15 have paved runways. Important airports in Sudan include Khartoum International Airport, Port Sudan, El Obeid, and Al Fashir.

The government-owned Sudan Railways operates the country's limited rail system. It serves mainly the more-populous northern and central regions. The main line runs from Wadi Halfa to Khartoum and southwest to El Obeid. It also passes to Nyala in southern Darfur and Waw in Bahr al-Ghazal. The rail connects Atbarah and Sannar with Port Sudan, and Sannar with Ad-Damazin, in addition to providing an 870-mile (1,400-km) line to the cotton-growing region of El Gezira.

MANUFACTURING

Before the extensive exportation of oil, most industry in Sudan consisted of food-processing plants around Khartoum, particularly plants processing cottonseed and peanut oil, wheat flour, raw sugar, and gum arabic. There are also factories producing cement, cotton textiles, glass, paper, and light machinery.

During the 1970s the government nationalized most industries and confiscated several foreign-owned firms, but this policy was reversed in the 1980s, and foreign investment is again encouraged. The introduction

A satellite image of the Shifa pharmaceutical plant.

Soap industry workers in Gedaref.

of Islamic law in 1983, which made it illegal to lend money at interest, confused the issue again. Large-scale industrial growth is also constrained by the underdeveloped and expensive transportation system, the inadequate infrastructure, and the lack of skilled manpower.

One industry that has been helping Sudan boost its export earnings is oil. Oil was discovered in the early 1980s in the South but not exploited until the late 1990s because of rebel activity. In August 1999 the government launched the strategically important 994-mile (1,600-km) pipeline that connects the oil field to a refinery on the Red Sea near Port Sudan. In 2003 the pipeline was extended another 373 miles (600 km), and oil production reached an estimated 300,000 barrels a day. Out of those, 200,000 barrels were exported, and about 70,000 barrels were consumed locally. Most of the petroleum is exported as crude, although some petroleum is refined for the local market. A 503-mile (810-km) line was constructed to carry the refined petroleum products. Currently other pipelines are under construction. One is the 870-mile (1,400-km) line linking the Melut Basin to an oil export terminal near Port Sudan;

another is a 110-mile (177-km) pipeline linking the Thar Jath and Mala fields also to Port Sudan.

MINING

Sudan is thought to have considerable natural resources of gold, iron ore, copper, zinc, tungsten, chromium, manganese, magnetite, salt, and mica, but because of political instability and difficult terrain, very little exploration or large-scale mining has been carried out. Gold has been mined for centuries in northern Sudan and the Red Sea Hills. The western region has vast untapped reserves of uranium. Chromite, a black ore from which chromium is extracted, exists near the Ethiopian border.

ENERGY

In 2000, Sudan's total installed electrical-generating capacity was rated at more than 2,500 megawatts, although actual production is less than capacity. Most towns have electricity for only a few hours a day. Outside of towns, electricity comes from small, individually owned gasoline-driven generators.

Nationally about 46 percent of Sudan's electricity comes from hydroelectric power stations, with more than 70 percent produced by the Roseires Dam on the Blue Nile. There are also thermal-energy power plants that burn refined petroleum imported from neighboring countries, particularly Saudi Arabia. As in so many other aspects of life in Sudan, there is enormous potential for development and self-sufficiency, including opportunities for further hydroelectric and solar power generation, but so far the government has had difficulty getting sufficient financing.

One hydroelectric construction set to better meet Sudan's electrical needs is the Merowe Dam Project. Located just below the Fourth Cataract at Merowe, this hydroelectric project, budgeted at about $1.2 billion, is expected to generate 1,250 megawatts of power to Khartoum, Port Sudan, Dongola, and Atbara. The construction of this project is due to be completed by 2008.

ENVIRONMENT

SUDAN HAS LONG BEEN described as a land of plenty. Decades ago its flora and fauna were thriving with a profusion of lions, rhinos, elephants, expansive savannas, and lush rain forests. Unfortunately years of colonial rule and civil strife have left a terrible mark on Sudan's once-thriving environment. Large-scale population movements, mismanagement of natural resources, and changing weather patterns have led to environmental degradation that may take years to reverse. Sudan's environmental concerns are wide ranging, from the indiscriminate hunting of wildlife to a lack of access to water. Although there are still inadequate checks in place to monitor these environmental concerns, Sudan has tried, with foreign aid, to preserve and conserve as much as possible, given that it has only just emerged from more than two decades of war.

WILDLIFE

Sudan hosts an astonishing variety of wildlife. Out of 13 mammalian orders in Africa, 12 can be found living in Sudan. Because of its varied wildlife, Sudan generates significant revenue through tourism and sport hunting. Before the outbreak of the civil war, Sudan was known among African countries as the region with the most abundant game and wildlife tourism. Popular stretches for hunting are in the area between the Red Sea Hills and the Nubian Desert. From October to February, game such as the Nubian ibex, the Eritrean and Sommering gazelle, and the baboon are hunted. In the western desert, the hunting season lasts from September through February, with addaxes, Barbary sheep, red-fronted gazelles, ostriches, and white oryx being hunted. Birds such as ducks, bustards, guinea fowls, and doves are hunted from October to January.

For Sudan the economic value of allowing controlled sport hunting far outweighs its environmental drawbacks, as sport hunting brings in millions

Opposite: **Burial mounds and the bones of a dead animal in the desert. Severe droughts in Sudan have led to damages in the environment, like rapid desertification, and the death of people, plants, and livestock.**

There are about 971 species of bird, 106 species of fish, 15 species of amphibian, 162 species of mammal, including at least 34 species of antelope, and 302 species of reptile in Sudan.

51

of dollars in local income. However, the main cause of extinction of wild animals in Sudan is the country's inability to sustain the reproduction of its hunted wildlife. Currently about 20 species of fauna are threatened in Sudan. Sudan has also often been accused of blatant attempts to poach endangered species such as elephants and rhinos to promote an illegal ivory trade regardless of the international ban in 1989. In February 2005 an international conservation group allegedly discovered more than 11,000 ivory trinkets, ranging from pendants to cigarette holders, openly on sale in Khartoum. The easy availability of firearms, especially in the South, has also contributed to the excessive hunting of wildlife.

Sudan contends that some wildlife is destructive to humans and their livestock, crops, and property. A species of bird called the red-billed quelas has been destroying cereal crops, costing Sudan millions in potential revenue annually. Sudan's drilling for oil and the construction of oil pipelines in the South have also caused the fragmentation and loss of habitats.

Sudan's struggling economy and uncertain political climate have made the implementation of any major conservation initiatives rather difficult. Nevertheless, Sudan has made efforts in preservation by designating about 38,610 square miles (100,000 square km) of national parks and game reserves for wildlife protection. Its six major national parks cover a total area of 23,308 square miles (60,370 square km), and its 19 game reserves cover more than 13,706 square miles (35,500 square km), protecting about 5 percent of Sudan's total land area.

Sudan also has numerous environmental bodies to ensure some degree of conservation and preservation of wildlife. A leading nongovernmental organization is the Sudanese Environment Conservation Society (SECS), established in 1975, with 104 branches throughout Sudan. Aside from SECS, the Higher Council of the Environment and Natural Resources ensures that the appropriate authorities follow up on long-term plans for conservation and a sustainable use of natural resources. Other environmental bodies include the Wildlife Research Center, the Wildlife and Environment Conservation Administration, the National Research Center, the Remote Sensing Authority, and the Plan Sudan Organization. Universities in Sudan also play important roles in promoting environmental conservation and awareness.

WATER AND SANITATION

Although Sudan has around 4,942 million acres (2,000 million ha) of surface water, including the 4,145-mile (6,670-km) stretch of the Nile and its tributaries, the people of Sudan struggle to have an adequate supply of potable water. This problem is particularly pronounced in the South, where it is estimated that fewer than 30 percent of the population has access to safe water. For years the civil war hindered the building of a proper infrastructure for water and sanitation. Schools and hospitals often have to make do with inadequate facilities. Compared with 50 percent of urban dwellers, only 24 percent of the rural population has access to adequate sanitation facilities, such as a connection to a sewer or a septic tank system or even a simple pit latrine. Often there are no toilets or

A Sudan Liberation Army rebel drinks water taken from a wadi. The lack of access to safe water means that the Sudanese constantly face the risk of waterborne diseases.

modern water facilities in schools, and schoolchildren usually have to carry their own supply of water from home and perform bodily functions in areas surrounding the schools.

The return of more than 2 million internally displaced people is expected to further exacerbate the water issue, as more people will fight for the limited access to water and sanitation. The problem is compounded by drought and the discharge of silt from dams. The silt ends up blocking the Nile water currents, decreasing the volume of water flow and making Sudanese rivers open to invasion of weeds and waterborne diseases. The neglected infrastructure of the rainwater drainage system has also given rise to incidences of malaria, especially during the rainy season.

Aside from the threat to human health, inadequate access to safe water and sanitation will inhibit agriculture and animal husbandry and degrade the land with sewage. In Darfur inadequate water and appalling sanitation conditions, where raw sewage mingled with water sources, have resulted in outbreaks of cholera and diarrhea. Furthermore, what few wells and water systems exist in Darfur are either in disrepair or made inoperable by the ongoing conflict.

To address the issue in Darfur, a drilling rig was purchased to provide potable water for the internally displaced. Plans are in place to install new hand pumps and water tanks to accommodate more than 2 million people. The Sustainable Community Water Management Committee has also been formed, boring more than 40 holes to provide water for the general population in Sudan. Another initiative to improve access to sustainable safe water is the Water for Recovery and Peace Program (WRAPP), with emphasis on the Bahr al-Ghazal, Nuba Mountains, Upper Nile, and South Blue Nile regions. Under the School Sanitation and Hygiene Education (SSHE) Project, UNICEF together with the Ministry of Education and the National Water Corporation have already successfully provided some school areas in the South with water supplies, sanitation facilities, and hygiene education.

DESERTIFICATION

Some of the main causes of deforestation in Sudan, leading to desertification, are the harvesting of firewood, the overgrazing of animals, and drought. Between 1990 and 2005, Sudan lost about 11 percent of its forests. Darfur particularly is experiencing major deforestation. The population's dependence on wood and charcoal for its cooking needs has led to competition for scarce natural resources. Approximately 60 percent of Darfur's population depends on wood, going through 3,700 square miles (9,583 square km) of forests annually. The deforestation problem is so severe that some people have resorted to digging under the earth for roots.

Grasslands cover approximately two-thirds, or 600,000 square miles (1,553,993 square km), of Sudan. Unfortunately agricultural mismanagement has led to rampant overgrazing and the disappearance of several grasses and herbs including *Blepharis linariifolia* and *Cadaba farinosa* in many areas. As more areas are expanded to accommodate agricultural developments such as irrigation schemes and rainland crops, areas available to nomads for grazing will become even more limited. Yet the demand for meat, cheese, and milk is greater than ever with the increasing number of refugees.

The white oryx, the addax, and the trophy antelope, once common in the western desert, are now rarely seen.

There has been little reforestation effort, as awareness is weak among the majority of the public and the policymakers. The civil war also made reforestation difficult due to differing environmental policies. The annual rate of deforestation in Sudan is close to 1,245,411 acres (504,000 ha), yet only 74,132 acres (30,000 ha) have been reforested. Deforestation affects not only people's potential means of livelihood, as poor soil conditions cannot sustain crops, but also wildlife by destroying their habitats.

Several forest legislations have been issued, although the infrastructure for enforcing these laws is lacking. A lot of planning is needed to sustain healthy forest biodiversity. Improper land use has been identified, and the government has appointed the Forests National Corporation (FNC) to provide a balanced supply of forest goods and services to the population. Attempts at reforestation include planting trees as windbreaks around villages in the North, encouraging seedling nurseries, and promoting the growing of fruit-tree orchards in the South. Sudan's National Action Plan to Combat Desertification (SNAP) is left in charge to cover the problem of desertification for most of the land's desert or semidesert regions. International agencies have also helped by curbing the population's excessive need for firewood. They introduced the fuel-efficient stove program, in which stoves made from water, mud, and donkey dung reduce the need for firewood by 50 percent.

DROUGHT

One of the major obstacles to Sudan's securing a permanent livelihood from agriculture and livestock is that the country suffers from periodic droughts. Sudan's low rainfall, around 4–8 inches (100–200 mm) in some areas, has severely hurt agricultural production and depleted water resources. Since the infamous drought of 1985-86 that brought famine to the land, Sudan has been at the mercy of the weather, with droughts in 1989, 1990, 1997, and 2000 as well. Each time, crops would fail, and livestock and land for pasture would be lost. This is because many of Sudan's water yards and water pumps are nonfunctional. Desertification, already a problem, has been exacerbated by the droughts.

Droughts destabilize the population and break down traditional agricultural and livestock practices. Kordofan in western Sudan, the Darfur regions, and parts of central Sudan are usually the worst hit. Although all the causes of such extreme weather conditions are not clear, some scientists have pointed to deforestation and global warming as a few of the main causes.

While it may be possible for Sudan to combat regional desertification, the causes of global warming are largely international. Sudan for its part has signed and ratified several climate-change protocols aimed at reducing and releasing only acceptable levels of greenhouse gases into the atmosphere. The government has also made the best of this difficult situation by improving data-collection and early-warning systems in the Red Sea region. This will facilitate a quick-response system on modes of assistance when the next drought strikes. Other measures to reduce the effects of drought include upgrading water-harvesting techniques and educating rural communities on how to save their supplies for the days when there is no rain. The Turra water dam project is one example of conserving and channeling water. Located in North Darfur, the dam's reservoir can store up to 71,937 cubic yards (55,000 cubic m) of water, benefiting about 4,000 people, including nomadic herders in the area with their 8,000 goats, 400 sheep, 1,000 camels, 6,000 donkeys, and 100 horses.

A drought in Malleet, Northern Darfur, since 1997 has reduced the area to nothing more than a desert, causing the death of many livestock, wildlife, and flora.

SUDANESE

SUDAN IS AN INTERESTING PLACE in part because it is a point where diverse peoples meet. In the South the people are Nilotic Africans who live lives similar to people elsewhere in Africa, worshiping animist gods, living in mud-walled huts, farming, and gathering food as their ancestors did. Some people prefer to wear nothing but jewelry. And many are also Christian.

As one travels north the round, mud-walled houses give way to mud-brick one-story buildings with walled courtyards. Dress undergoes a total change, as nudity or light clothing gradually gives way to complete covering. Muslims consider it irreligious to have exposed flesh, so men wear long white robes and turbans, while women wear full-length dresses covered by a wrap that leaves only their faces exposed.

Left: **Women attend a nutrition class.**

Opposite: **Sudanese children crowd around to take a picture in front of their school.**

PEOPLE OF THE NORTH

Around 40 percent of Sudanese people consider themselves to be Arab, although a much larger proportion speak Arabic and live an Arabic lifestyle. Some of those who call themselves Arabs are descendants of Arabs who emigrated to Sudan, while others belong to Sudanese groups who fully adopted Arabic language and culture. The Arabs live chiefly in northern Sudan, in settled communities and extended families rather than in nomadic groups. They consider the home a very private place, but they are also very hospitable and freely offer strangers a rest and a meal. Arab people fill all walks of life in Sudan, from small farmers to city intellectuals. Main Arab tribes in Sudan include the Ja'alayin, the

A Nubian child tends goats on the banks of the Nile.

Juhayna, and the Shagia. The Juhayna are nomadic, while the Ja'alayin are agriculturalists. The Juhayna have two subgroups, the Kabbabish and the Baggara. The Shagia are partly nomadic and partly agriculturists. Although they originally lived only in northern Sudan, today they can be found throughout the country.

The other major group in northern Sudan is the Nubian peoples, who represent around 8 percent of the population of Sudan. They speak Nubian, an ancient language with its own alphabet and literature. Modern Nubians also speak Arabic. Many were resettled in other areas of Sudan after the Aswan Dam flooded their land. They are gradually

A Nubian village of Sesebi in Upper Nubia.

becoming assimilated into Arab culture. In appearance they are close to their Arab neighbors, with straight black hair and slightly darker skin.

PEOPLE OF THE WEST

The mountains of southern Kordofan are home to the Nuba, a dark-skinned group of tribes, some of whom are Muslim. Farther to the west are people such as the settled Fur, a Muslim group after whom the Darfur provinces are named; the Baggara tribes, who are nomadic traders; and the Zaghawa, who are also nomads. The Zaghawa regularly make the enormous trek across the desert to the Libyan border. There they sell their great herds of camels and trade in salt, a rare commodity in Sudan. The Fallata people, across Sudan, are unlike any of their neighbors and are thought to have descended from the Fulani group, a Muslim nomadic tribe from northern Nigeria.

BAGGARA TRIBES

The Baggara tribes are nomads who claim Arab descent. By the 16th century nomadic Arabs from northern Africa and Arabia had migrated as far as Lake Chad and had intermarried with Africans. In the 18th century their descendants moved to Sudan, where the land was suited to their nomadic lifestyle.

Traditionally they have a social system based on family ties, changing allegiances, and blood feuds. Power is not hereditary but stems from wealth and strength of personality. Many Baggara groups today live in central Sudan. The major tribes include the Rizeigat, the Ta'isha, and the Habbaniya in Darfur and the Homr, the Messiria, and the Hawazma in Kordofan.

THE NUBA

The story of the Nuba people is a 20th-century tragedy. They inhabit the Nuba Mountains in Kordofan. For centuries the 50 groups that make up the Nuba lived peacefully among themselves and with their Arab neighbors. They kept cattle and terraced the mountainsides to grow grain, vegetables, and fruit. Many of them practiced an unconventional form of Islam that allowed alcohol and pork, but there were sometimes Christians and animists within the same family. They went for the most part naked.

During the 1970s and 1980s many tourists came to the area to see their traditional dances and wrestling. The government began a campaign to clothe the Nuba and force them to follow traditional Islamic rules. After several years of persecution the Nuba declared their support for the SPLA, and since then the policy of "civilizing" the Nuba has given way to eradication. The Nuba Mountains have been cut off from the rest of the world, and government troops have carried out a scorched-earth policy, killing and burning the Nuba's crops and animals. Whole groups have been forced into camps where men and women are segregated, and there have been reports of rape and genocide.

By 1999 more than 100,000 Nuba had been displaced. The signing of the Burgenstock Agreement in 2002 calling for ceasefire in the Nuba Mountains between the government and the SPLA has given the Nuba people some semblance of normality. The peace protocol signed three years later was meant in part to ensure significant autonomy for the people.

Since the early 1990s approximately 25,000 Nuer and Dinka have resettled in the U.S. as refugees to escape the civil war.

PEOPLE OF THE EAST

The Rashaida are a nomadic tribe of people who arrived in the Sudan region from Saudi Arabia in the early 19th century. They live in goatskin tents in the area around Kassala. They are easily recognizable by the heavy veils and silver jewelry worn by the women and the colorful turbans worn by the men.

When a girl from the Rashaida tribe is ready to marry, she approaches the man she wants and flirtatiously lifts her veil so that he can see her chin. If he accepts her offer he must find 100 camels for her bride price. By tradition the Rashaida breed camels and goats, but in modern times many of them drive Toyota trucks.

The Beja are Muslims living in the Red Sea Hills. They became famous in Britain in the 19th century for their fierce fighting in the Mahdist battles. Although they are traditionally nomadic, some Beja have adopted a lifestyle of farming cotton. They regard the sea as hostile and do not eat fish except in times of extreme need. The major Beja groups are the Bisharin, the Hadendowa, the Amarar, the Ababda, and the Beni Amer. Their thick, curly hair gives them quite a distinctive appearance, and those who work on the docks in Port Sudan are distinguishable by their traditional hairstyles.

PEOPLE OF THE SOUTH

The Dinka are the largest non-Arab ethnic group in southern Sudan, making up 20 percent of the southern population. They are traditional nomadic herders whose lives revolve around their animals. Fiercely independent, they saw the introduction of shariah law as an attack on their way of life. While many of them try to live peacefully, many more

Opposite: **The heavily decorated veil identifies this woman as a member of the Rashaida tribe.**

Below: **Refugees at Wadi Sherifa. The political conflict in Sudan has lead to many homeless southern Sudanese.**

became soldiers of the SPLA living deep in the southern forests, raiding other ethnic groups for food, shelter, and clothes and threatening all road and air transport. Most of their rebel activities came to a halt, however, when the SPLA successfully brokered a deal with the government in 2005 giving the people significant regional autonomy and exception to the shariah law.

Neutral people have also been displaced by the war. The Mundari, who lived just south of the Sudd, were attacked by cattle-raiding Dinka and government troops in the mid-1980s and fled south to refugee camps

ETHNIC GROUPS AND THEIR CATTLE

Cattle herding is not just a job for the people of the South. Cattle are their currency and provide food, drink, clothing, and fuel.

A Dinka's social status is determined by the number of animals in his herd. Each year the tribes move their cattle back and forth between the river and the grasslands. When a Dinka boy comes of age he is given his first ox and takes a name determined by the appearance of the ox. The Dinka even make up songs about their cattle.

Before the Mundari were displaced by the war, looking after cattle dominated their lives. Their cattle are huge and have thick branched horns that the Mundari train to grow into intricate shapes.

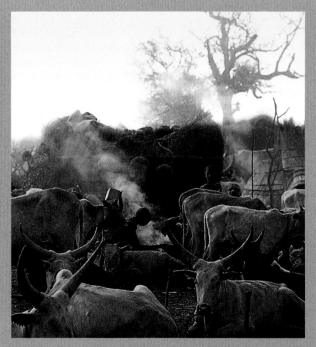

around Juba. Some of them have taken to self-defense and carry automatic weapons. The chance of their ancient way of life surviving the war is very remote.

The Shilluk are an animist group who has farmed the fertile banks of the Nile south of Khartoum since the 16th century. The king of the Shilluk, called a *reth* (RAY-th), is a living symbol of the spirit of Nyikang, the first Shilluk king and cultural hero. The *reth* wields considerable political power. Other southerners include the Nuer, the Bari, the Achole, and the Azande.

DRESS

There can be no more-radical differences in dress than those that exist in Sudan.

A Shilluk war dance. Despite Western and Arabic influences, traditional practices remain strong in many tribes of the South.

In the cities of the North and the South, business is conducted in Western or Arab dress, usually a thin short-sleeve shirt and cotton trousers for men and a light cotton dress with a *tobe* (TOH-bay) for women. A *tobe* is a 10-yard (9-m) piece of thin fabric. It is wrapped around and around the body, covering its outlines and leaving only the face exposed. Men wear ties and jackets on formal occasions.

At home and on the streets, men from the North relax in the loose, long cotton shirt called a *jallabiya* (CHAL-a-bee-ah), loose pants, and a turban called an *imma* (EM-ah). They are also likely to wear this dress for formal occasions.

Inside the house, many northern women wear Western clothes that are longer and cover more of the body than their Western peers might want to wear in such a climate. Out of the house they cover this with a *tobe*. A *tobe*'s color is chosen to match the clothes underneath. For work a white *tobe* is worn, while women in eastern Sudan often wear black *tobe*. In some areas in the west and far north the *tobe* are very colorful.

Women can be arrested for appearing in public dressed immodestly. This law becomes more relaxed the farther south one travels.

Traditionally the southern people wear little except jewelry. Some (particularly older women) wear beaded aprons or sarongs and practice facial scarring. However, both the near-nudity and the facial scarring are in rapid decline.

REFUGEES

The second civil war in Sudan killed nearly 2 million people and displaced 4 million more. Those displaced have since left for Chad and Egypt and some even to Asia and Europe. The ongoing conflict in Darfur has displaced even more Sudanese. In Kalma, Darfur's biggest refugee camp, more than 150,000 people are dependent on food aid.

Refugee camps in central and southern Sudan are filled with Sudanese people displaced by the war, as well as with refugees from Chad, Uganda, and other African countries.

SCARRING

Scarring is a very ancient tradition in Sudan. Frescoes in the historical city of Meroë depict scarring patterns on the faces of people. Scarification is a major ethnic and aesthetic component not only among the southern people in Sudan but also across other parts of Africa. Sometimes scarification is performed on girls to mark the stages of life process, such as puberty or marriage. Men also have facial scarring, which is carried out as part of their initiation into manhood.

A common scarring pattern among the Shilluk is a row of raised bumps across the forehead, made by rubbing ash into the wounds. The Shilluk king has this type of scarring. The Nuer have six parallel lines on their foreheads, while the Ja'alayin have lines marked on their cheeks. The scarring is, to them, considered beautiful and identifies ethnicities.

Other forms of body decoration include lip tattooing, practiced by some women in the North, and painting hands and feet with intricate henna patterns.

Because of government campaigns and the influence of missionaries, many southern people now wear clothes. The government policy of clothing the southern people became part of the conflict between the North and the South. Southerners resent the attempts to impose Islamic laws and customs on their traditional lifestyles, while the people of the North believe that it is their religious duty to encourage the spread of Islam.

LIFESTYLE

IT IS VERY UNLIKELY that anyone in Sudan has been unaffected by the calamities of the past decade. A large portion of the population is nomadic at least part of the year, and it is perhaps these people who have been hardest hit by the years of drought and the rapid encroachment of the desert. Farmers living along the fertile banks of the Nile experienced a serious flood in the mid-1980s that did enormous damage to their homes and herds. They have also been raided by both SPLA and government troops. Groups such as the Nuba have been the most affected, with their very existence in danger. The general economic slump, the upholding of shariah law in the North, and the many government coups have affected everyone who tries to make a living in the rural areas and in the cities. Until the government is politically and economically stable, there will be little improvement in basic social services to alleviate the suffering of the people.

The major divisions in lifestyle are those between the North and the South and between the city and the country.

People in the hot, dry North can make a living selling water carried from the wells. Many women and children spend a large portion of their day finding enough water to keep themselves and their animals alive.

Left: **A Dinka family pounds millet in front of their mud-and-straw hut.**

Opposite: **A Bedouin draws water from a well in the desert. Many Sudanese are nomads, making sure that their herds survive the harsh climate by driving them from one watering hole to the next.**

A busy street in Omdur-man. There are few wo-men to be seen on the streets of Sudan.

LIFE IN THE NORTH

During the long hot days, life in Sudanese cities is conducted at a slow pace. Many people in Khartoum live in modern Western-style apartment blocks with the ease of electricity and piped water. The city suffers from frequent power cuts, however, so refrigeration and air-conditioning are almost nonexistent. Most of the daily life of Khartoum is conducted out in the open under whatever shade is around. Wooden-frame string beds are pulled out of the house into the courtyard to serve as chairs.

In the city, life revolves around the souk, the city market. The Khartoum area's largest souk is in Omdurman, where craftworkers of all kinds make precious objects out of ivory, ebony, gold, and silver. More ordinary souks contain shops selling fresh food, tobacco, and a few electrical goods. Aside from souks, Sudanese also shop at Afra Mall, Sudan's first shopping mall, which opened in Khartoum in 2004. Covering an area of 35,880 square yards (30,000 square m), the mall offers three movie theaters, a hypermarket, a food court, an Internet café, and a bowling alley. Beauty salons and electronics and clothing stores are also featured at the mall.

Khartoum's city center has skyscrapers, some big hotels, and stores catering to the small number of tourists who venture this far south. Business hours are usually between 8 A.M. and 2 P.M. Everything closes during the afternoon and reopens again when it is cooler, from 6 P.M. to 8 P.M., Saturday through Thursday, with Friday as the day of rest. On Sunday, Christians are allowed two hours to attend church services should they desire to do so.

In the wealthier parts of the city the houses have high fences with carefully guarded four-wheel-drive cars parked outside. Inside the prize possessions are the television and the VCR. Wealthy families have several servants, who sleep out in the courtyard while the family sleeps inside.

Northern Sudanese villagers also live an Arab lifestyle, with thick-walled square houses built around a central courtyard. Most villages are on the banks of the Nile or at a few desert oases. Similar to life in the cities, village life occurs mostly outside during the day, in courtyards and at roadside tea shops. People work in the fields, tend their animals, and make goods for sale or barter.

Many Sudanese women supplement the family's income by selling goods in the market.

THE SOUK

All Sudanese towns have a marketplace known as the souk. It is usually the center of town both physically and socially. The souk is often a warren of streets in which it is easy to become lost.

The souk is divided into craft and merchandise sections—all the goldsmiths are in one part of the souk, while all the greengrocers are in another. The goldsmiths make jewelry in the back of the shop to sell at the front. Baskets and leather bags are sold here for daily use. Some souks sell only Western luxury items; others sell camels or donkeys in a separate animal souk. Throughout the souk are tea shops where hot, sweet mint tea can be drunk at one's leisure. These are popular places to meet friends and catch up on news and gossip.

NOMADIC LIFE

More than a tenth of the population of Sudan has a seminomadic or nomadic existence.

Different nomadic groups have different ways of life. The Rashaida in northeastern Sudan make their tents out of woven goat hair, while the tents of the nearby Hadendowa are made out of palm-fiber mats.

Many northern tribes herd livestock such as cattle, goats, and camels and wander the desert following the sudden rainstorms. After a storm a patch of desert that has been infertile for years will suddenly blossom and provide a temporary pasture for the vast herds of animals.

Other nomads are traders who make long journeys back and forth across the desert using trucks and, to a lesser extent, camel trains, bartering gold or salt for other goods.

BROKEN FAMILIES

The disruption in the traditional patterns of life in Sudan by war, floods, droughts, and famine has resulted in the breakup of traditional family units. Many men have had to leave their families and go in search of work, leaving Muslim women as head of the household for the first time in their lives. The women, however, have some means of income, through remittances and financial help by the extended family.

Sons also leave home at a very young age so as not to be a burden to their families. They go to the cities, where they quickly become beggars and thieves, sleeping in the streets and often receiving injuries in accidents. In Khartoum and Nyala there are programs to rehabilitate such children. They are taught a trade and encouraged to return to their homes.

LIFE IN THE SOUTH

As one travels farther south both the countryside and the people change. The indigenous population is African rather than Arab, and their lifestyle has little in common with that of their northern compatriots. People wear fewer clothes, and many decorate their bodies with scars.

The typical square, mud-brick houses give way to groups of round houses with mud walls and thatched straw roofs. The houses are arranged in circles around a swept, earthen courtyard where most of the village activities take place. Most people in rural Sudan live close to other members of their extended family. After his initiation ceremony, a boy will build his own home within the village compound. Cooking is done over an open fire, as most houses lack electricity. The lack of indoor plumbing means that water is drawn from nearby wells, rivers, or streams. The villages are often surrounded by grass walls to keep children in and wildlife out.

Beyond the houses are small fields irrigated once a year by the Nile floods. In the floodplains as many as three harvests a year can be made. Most families work to produce their own food and enough to barter for their other needs. Sometimes they sell their produce to middlemen, who often pay the villagers as little as possible. There are few paid jobs except for agricultural workers at harvest time.

Away from the floodplains people depend on wells for water. The government has drilled many wells and provided a complex series of irrigation canals. In recent years, because of the drain on Sudan's water

A Dinka wedding dance. The cattle are being given as dowry.

resources, wells have had to be drilled deeper and deeper before water could be found.

South of the Sudd the dependence on the river for irrigation stops, and the land is hot and verdant. Evidence of Western missionaries can be seen in the many clapboard churches and schools. The local people grow vegetables to sell in the North, keep cattle, and hunt game for food.

In more wooded and higher regions, houses are built of wood. People wear clothes to keep warm in the lower temperatures and use fires for heating as well as for cooking.

The recently ended war brought huge disruption to the lives of many southerners, with whole ethnic groups being displaced by raids from both sides. Even the current relative peace is still marred by gun battles between rival clans over cattle, pasture, and water.

WOMEN

Arab women are very carefully guarded by their families. They do not mix socially with men who are not their kin, and they cover themselves with long cloths when they go outside. Women tend to spend much more time in the home, while men take care of business outside the home (including doing the daily shopping). There are few Arab girls living on the streets in Sudan; no matter how poor a family is, it is a tenet of their faith that girls are weak and should be protected, and even very distant cousins will be taken in if they have no other means of support.

In the past few years, missionary institutions and other foreign aid organizations have been involved in the effort to distribute food to the war-torn South.

A girl is often married as a teenager to a man she might have met only a few times and may never have spoken to privately. Her husband pays a bride price to her parents.

Since the implementation of the 1998 constitution guaranteeing gender equality and the right of women to economic and political freedom, the restrictions placed on women have eased somewhat. Today there are about 70 women in the 450-person National Assembly and three as national state ministers.

Sudanese women are not only relatively well represented in public life, but many are also well educated. Women make up about 60 percent of university-enrolled students.

Roughly 58 percent of women cannot read or write, due to a lack of access to education.

It is estimated that 2.3 percent of Sudan's population is infected with AIDS. Sudan's first voluntary counseling and testing center was opened in Juba in February 2004, although it was feared that the Islamic reluctance to discuss sexual matters would hinder the population from getting the necessary help.

Like rural Arab women, many rural non-Arab women live a lifestyle different from that of city women. They work hard in the fields, collecting water, caring for animals, and making goods to sell. The Felata across Sudan believe that women should earn their own living. The girls are independent, and many work, selling sweetmeats in the marketplaces. They wear brightly colored clothes and jewelry. Those who get the opportunity attend school wearing shorts just like the boys in their class.

HEALTH CARE

For most periods since the early 20th century the Sudanese people have suffered from frequent epidemics of diseases such as meningitis, sleeping sickness, and yellow fever. The efforts of the Sudan Medical Service (later the Ministry of Health) and missionary institutions reduced the death rate, but the drought, the war of the 1980s and 1990s, and the current conflict in Darfur still resulted in reducing life expectancy. War, famine, and disease are the major causes of death, and life expectancy is only 58 years for men and 60 years for women. Infant mortality is around 61 deaths per thousand live births.

The civil war and the current conflict have diverted much-needed medical resources that would otherwise have gone into preventive health care and the training of professionals. Many valued medical professionals left Sudan to escape the war and seek employment elsewhere. It is estimated that there are only 22 doctors per 100,000 people. There are about 160 hospitals in Sudan, most of them in the cities. But they are poorly equipped and have poor standards of hygiene. There are roughly 7.2 beds per 10,000 people. Hospital services are free. There are also doctors in private practice in the larger towns.

In rural areas and the South, medical care is very basic. There is a severe shortage of local doctors, so most medical care is undertaken by

SELF-HELP FOR WOMEN

In rural areas many of the daily activities of finding, growing, and preparing food are done by women. Aid agencies have become aware of the important role that women play in the survival of families and have begun to educate women to make use of their informal and domestic skills.

In 1993 a women's group called Yed el Marra (Women's Hand) set up a grain mill in a remote village in South Darfur called Milebada. In villages like this, women spend much of the day grinding grain by hand or carrying it to the nearest town to be ground. After being trained to operate the new mill, they found that they saved time and money and could even earn a little money grinding grain for other villages. The small profits go toward local literacy and health projects. The mill is run by simple, easily replaced technology, so it does not depend on foreign technical help. More mills and training programs have been set up in other rural communities.

Another group in South Darfur, the Baketa Organization for Women and Children, was established to help women displaced from the Darfur conflict learn to become seamstresses. Over a period of three months, women are taught to mend and sew household items. In the fourth month, the women learn how to fix and maintain sewing machines. Incomes earned as seamstresses allow the women to purchase firewood in local markets. Skill-building programs such as this are common in Darfur's camps. They not only help women earn much-needed income, but they also help prevent the women from being vulnerable to attacks when they leave home to gather firewood or work in the fields. The first batch of 85 students graduated in February 2006, with the second class of more than 60 students already under way.

foreign aid workers and midwives with very basic training. Sometimes the people in the rural areas depend on folk remedies that are limited in their effectiveness.

Only 69 percent of the population has access to safe water and sanitary facilities. Combined with the scarcity of medicines, many people die of easily preventable diseases such as measles and dysentery. Spending on

A MUSLIM WEDDING

A traditional Sudanese Muslim wedding lasts about three days. Once it would have lasted up to 40 days, but that custom is no longer followed. Before the pair is betrothed, a good deal of bargaining goes on between the families of the bride and the groom, who may be related anyway. The groom must pay a bride price to the bride's father in addition to bestowing a dowry on the bride herself.

As the wedding approaches it is customary for the girl to feign unhappiness. She may stop eating and look sad. Her body is oiled and perfumed, and all body hair except that on her head is removed using boiled sugar and lemon juice. Her hands are painted with henna in intricate floral patterns.

The night before the wedding, the groom holds a party in the courtyard. A feast is set out, and men and women sit in separate groups to eat. After the food come speeches and dancing. The men dance first, in swaying, stamping rows. The women dance in groups of two or three, joining and stopping while the men dance continuously. While the dancing goes on, the groom walks around the groups of people waving a stick and shouting; the others shout back or howl at him.

The ceremony itself is carried out the following day by an imam (Muslim leader) in the presence of the parents. The bride and the groom do not take part. Seven women go down to the Nile and throw food in, returning with water to wash the bride's face. That night the bride's family holds another party. The bride dances for the groom and guests. (*pictured below, a wedding in Omdurman.*)

health care is low—only 1 percent of the country's GDP. However, the percentage of children immunized against most major childhood diseases had risen to approximately 60 percent by the late 1990s from very low rates in earlier decades. Diseases such as malaria, river blindness, hepatitis A, and tuberculosis remain endemic in the Nile Valley.

EDUCATION

Sudan technically provides eight years of free compulsory education, from ages 6 to 14, but in reality the policy is not strictly enforced, and many rural and displaced children

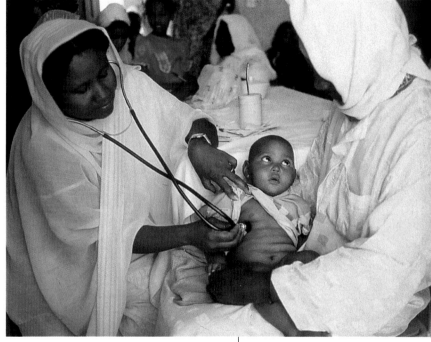

A man brings his child to a doctor in Khartoum.

have no schools to attend. In 2000 only 53 percent of Sudan's children attended during the "compulsory" years. Today only 21 percent of 14-year-olds attend school, and only 6.1 percent are educated beyond the age of 18. Ten percent of girls ages 7 to 14 attend school, and out of that only 1 percent finish primary education. In southern Sudan close to 90 percent of all women are illiterate. Although these figures are dismal, they are an improvement from previous generations, when only 9 percent of people over the age of 35 had any education at all. The country's current literacy rate stands at 61 percent. Sudan's weak economy has made improving the educational system difficult. Often the teachers are poorly qualified, and the better ones are lost to better-paying nations.

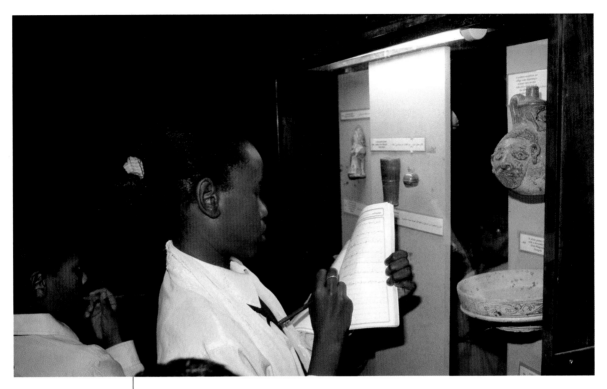

Sudanese children on an educational field trip to a museum in Khartoum. Both boys and girls have opportunities to attend school.

There are two levels of schools: basic (6 to 14 years old) and secondary (14 to 17 years old). The primary language of instruction is Arabic, although English is offered as a foreign language in grades 7 through 11. The school year runs from July to March.

Sudan has more than 40 institutions of higher learning and technical training colleges throughout the country, including those in Khartoum, Omdurman, and Juba.

FAMINE

For much of the 20th century, the lifestyle of many Sudanese was dominated by the need to find food. Although Sudan is rich in fertile agricultural land and mineral resources, population displacement from the war and recurrent droughts have given rise to widespread malnutrition outside the central Nile region.

In 1984 and 1985 western Sudan around Kordofan and Darfur and eastern Sudan near Kassala experienced unprecedented droughts. Roughly

400,000 people from Kordofan came to central Sudan in search of food and water for their animals. Seven million people suffered from malnutrition and came close to starvation, and many died. The problem was made worse by temperatures of 126°F (52°C) and ferocious sandstorms.

A second wave of famine, this time caused by the war, hit Sudan in 1989. By this time a relief infrastructure was in place with various aid agencies supplying food, but both the government and the SPLA caused problems, with neither side wanting the other to receive the aid. Much of the aid went to government troops rather than to the citizens of the North or the South, where around 2.6 million people were in need of emergency aid. In some areas of the South, 60 percent of the people suffered from malnutrition.

As the nation struggles to recover from the war, the raging ethnic warfare in the Darfur region sees an estimated 2.7 million people, including 1.8 million children, at risk from malnutrition and requiring food assistance. The ongoing insecurity in the region has deterred farmers from cultivating crops for fear of attacks. To make matters worse, in May 2006 the UN World Food Program decreased food aid to Sudan due to the lack of donor funds. The minimum daily requirement was halved from 2,100 calories to 1,050 calories per person to feed about 350,000 people dying from malnutrition and disease.

A villager in Kordofan uses a thumbprint to sign for sorghum.

RELIGION

IT IS ESTIMATED THAT SEVENTY percent of Sudan's population is Muslim, 25 percent practice indigenous religions or syncretic faiths, and 5 percent are Christian.

ISLAM

The word *Islam* means "submission." Muslims believe in the word of God and submit to all his words as handed down by the prophets. Islam acknowledges as prophets several figures out of Christianity and Judaism, including Abraham (Ibrahim), Adam, Noah, Moses, and Jesus. Muslims believe that Jesus is merely one of the prophets who have heard the word of God, rather than the son of God.

The most recent and revered of the prophets is Muhammad (A.D. 507–632). His following grew, and after his death most of Arabia converted to Islam. Muhammad's birthplace, Mecca in Saudi Arabia, became the religion's holy

The third pillar of faith is to give 2.5 percent of one's income to the poor. In Sudan, as in most other Arab countries, this is no longer an enforced law but is left to the conscience or compassion of the individual.

THE FIVE PILLARS OF FAITH

Muslims must carry out five acts of faith, namely:
- *Shahada* (SHAH-ha-da)—the first pillar of Islam, according to which believers must publicly declare that there is no God but Allah and that Muhammad is his prophet or messenger.
- *Solat* (soh-lat)—in reference to prayers carried out five times a day, at sunrise, noon, midafternoon, sunset, and night.
- *Zakat* (zah-kat)—the giving of alms to the poor.
- *Puasa* (pua-sah)—the act of fasting during the holy month of Ramadan.
- Hajj—a pilgrimage to Mecca that is to be made at least once in a Muslim's lifetime.

Opposite: **The Great Mosque area in Khartoum. Most Northern Sudanese are Muslims.**

Devout Muslims pray five times a day, even when at work.

Apostasy (conversion) from Islam to Christianity is a capital offense in Sudan.

city because it was there that the first mosque was built. It is called the Kaaba and contains a black stone believed to have been given to Ibrahim by the archangel Gabriel. God's words were collected by Muhammad into a holy book called the Koran (or Qur'an).

ISLAMIC WORSHIP Muslims make a commitment to pray five times a day. At each of the prayer times the muezzin calls the faithful to the mosque. Before praying the devotee removes his or her shoes and holds them in the left hand. The body is carefully washed according to ritual and in a certain order. The devotee faces the direction of Mecca and goes through a ritual of standing, bowing, and sitting, reciting prescribed prayers as he or she does so. The prayers should be carried out in a congregation, but if people cannot attend a mosque they can say their prayers alone. On Fridays there are special prayers in all mosques.

FASTING Fasting is required of all Muslims during the month of Ramadan. Besides refraining from eating and drinking from dawn to dusk during Ramadan, they must also abstain from smoking and other worldly desires. In addition, if they can afford it they must feed poor people. The fast can be delayed if one is sick, pregnant, or on a hazardous journey.

PILGRIMAGE Every Muslim who can afford it is obligated to make the journey to Mecca at least once in his or her lifetime. For thousands of Arab people that once meant a vast journey of several months across the Libyan and Nubian deserts in a camel train. The pilgrimage must be made in a state of grace, and strict rules have to be observed. Pilgrims have to be in a state of ritual purity, bathing in a special fluid and wearing a seamless white garment. The pilgrims must not cut their hair or nails, engage in marital relations, or shed blood. Once the pilgrims arrive at Mecca, they have to perform a number of rites in a specific order. The rites include running between the tops of Mount Marwah and Mount Safa seven times and stoning the three pillars at Mina, signifying the devil, with seven consecutive pebbles.

The Egyptian Mosque in Khartoum is one of Sudan's most famous landmarks.

ISLAMIC LAW Islamic law includes both legal and moral concepts. Many of the rules of Islamic law cannot be put into a legal system and must be a matter of conscience.

The laws of Islam are laid down in the Koran and the Sunna, which is a code of conduct for Muslims to follow, and have been added to by various religious groups over many centuries. They uphold the importance of the family and declare men and women to be equal, except that men are "a degree higher." The Koran forbids infanticide of girls, which was once common among the Arab tribes; allocates a degree of inheritance

Pilgrims waiting to depart for Mecca.

Muslim and local religious traditions coexist among the Fur people. They splash sanctuaries with a paste made of flour and water to ensure fertility and make sacrifices at shrines when the rains are likely to fall. The office of rainmaker is hereditary.

to girls; and describes the treatment of wives. Women are given the right of divorce in the case of ill treatment, but adultery is proscribed, with a punishment of 100 lashes. Under Islamic law men are allowed to marry up to four wives and can divorce any wife at will. Other important laws of Islam forbid eating pork and drinking alcohol.

JIHAD Etymologically, *jihad* means "struggle" or "strive." However, there are many interpretations of the word. It is most commonly interpreted as striving toward spiritual self-perfection or a war waged against the enemies of Islam. Nevertheless, it must be noted that the Koran does not condone the arbitrary use of violence but as a last resort.

ANIMISM

Animist religions are the most ancient religions practiced in Sudan, particularly in the Nilotic South. Animists believe that the natural objects around them have spiritual power and are able to influence their lives in many ways. Many animist groups worship one particular totem such as a wild animal, a particular tree, or a river and will do anything to avoid injuring that entity.

Most animist societies worship their ancestors, believing that the spirits of their ancestors must be carefully looked after because they have the power to bring harm or good to the family. Because each group respects the rights of other groups to worship their own ancestors, the various animist religions have never been in conflict, although people have fought for other reasons.

Many people also believe in the evil eye: a menacing look or glare from a person with magical powers or the help of a witch that could cause them harm. As such, many people wear amulets to protect themselves from such curses, and small babies are kept well away from public view in case someone sees them and puts the evil eye on them.

TRADITIONAL MEDICINE

The aid groups who have gone to Sudan to help with the refugee crises, famines, and floods recorded some of the local beliefs, especially those concerning medicine. One traditional cure for certain illnesses is to burn the victim with hot nails to drive out the illness, while a cure for malaria

is to make 44 cuts on the patient's body. The Fallata in western Sudan have *faki* (FAY-ki), who are part teachers/scholars and part magicians. For one month each year the *faki* collect herbs and roots that they make into spells and potions to cure illnesses or arouse the interest of a potential lover.

CHRISTIANITY

Nubia had three kingdoms for centuries before the advent of Islam. Many religious orders are still active in Sudan, although the kind of evangelical Christianity that has taken hold in much of the rest of Africa is not so prevalent here. Most of Sudan's Catholics are in the South. Great cathedrals built by missionaries still exist, and there are still missions operating schools and hospitals in the South. The rhythms of African music have influenced religious meetings all over the country.

LANGUAGE

MORE THAN 100 languages and 400 dialects are spoken in Sudan. Many of these languages are spoken by quite tiny numbers of people.

The main language is a form of Arabic spoken throughout the country. Arabic began its rise to prominence in the 14th century, and its position was established when it was made the official language of the government of the Funj sheikhdom, the Mahdist state, and early colonial governments. In the South the language of the Dinka people, whose five major dialects are collectively known as Jaang, is a lingua franca (common language) used among local people. English once had an official role in the country, and many people still speak it, especially in the South, where English missionaries established schools.

Most Sudanese speak at least two or three languages. These include their mother tongue, Arabic, and some English, as well as a smattering of other local languages.

Opposite: **A crowd gathers around a man holding the newspaper. Even though most Sudanese can speak a number of languages, many cannot read.**

THE LANGUAGE OF ANCIENT MEROË

A written language has existed in ancient Sudan since the third millennium B.C. Egyptian rulers left inscriptions on their tombs in Sudan written in Egyptian hieroglyphics. The African civilization that created the city of Meroë had its own written script (*pictured here*), which was stylistically but not etymologically related to ancient Egyptian. The Meroitic script was first recorded in writing in the second century B.C. The script has two forms, hieroglyphic and cursive. The Meroitic hieroglyphic signs were borrowed from the Egyptians, while the cursive script is derived mainly from the Egyptian demotic script.

In this village with no classroom, Arabic is taught outside under a shady tree.

ARABIC

Arabic is the major language in Sudan, spoken either as a mother tongue or as a lingua franca among groups of other language speakers. The standard form of Arabic from Saudi Arabia, called classical Arabic, is the official language and is used in official documents, as well as on formal occasions. However, very few people use it regularly. This causes some educational problems, since it is the official language of education and the language in which textbooks are printed.

Most urban residents, pastoralists, and farmers in the North and in the center of the country speak a unique form of Arabic that has developed in Sudan. It is mutually intelligible to some extent with Egyptian Arabic but has some differences. Sudanese Arabic is spoken by 21 million people in Sudan and is the language of trade.

In the South, Juba Arabic, a creole, or pidgin language, has developed. This creole is similar to Sudanese Arabic but could not be understood by an Egyptian. It is the first language of about 21,000 people in the area around Juba and south into Equatoria, and about 64,000 people speak it as their second language. It replaces Arabic as the lingua franca in the far South. It is the language of trade and the language that many schoolteachers use unofficially in the classroom. Political figures have also been known to use Juba Arabic to address ethnically mixed audiences.

The three forms of Arabic used in Sudan are only partly mutually intelligible, in the same way that Spanish and Portuguese speakers can understand a little of what a speaker of the other language is saying. All three forms of the language are tonal, which means that they use intonation to change the meaning of a word. The same groups of letters said in different tones have completely different meanings.

WRITTEN ARABIC

Arabic script, written from right to left, is based on a different system from that of the Roman alphabet. The Roman alphabet is not able to describe all the sounds in Arabic, nor can it represent the tones. Although written Arabic is somewhat similar to written Sudanese Arabic, some Arabic script cannot represent the actual words used by Sudanese creole speakers.

The number of people who use Juba Arabic or another Arabic creole as a first or second language is increasing all the time at the expense of English, which is gradually going out of use.

GREETINGS AND BODY LANGUAGE

It is common when greeting someone in Arabic to touch one's heart and say, "*Is Salaam aleyakum*" (Is sah-LAHM ah-LAY-ah-koom; "Peace be with you"), followed by "*Kayf halak*" (KYFE hah-LAHK) or "*Kaefak*" (Ka-A-fak; "How are you?")

The right hand is held out in a formal handshake between strangers, although a man will never touch a woman unless the woman offers her hand first. Often men will embrace each other in a hug on greeting, but men and women rarely embrace in this way.

As in many other Muslim countries, use of the left hand is avoided as much as possible. Objects are passed between people with either the right hand or both hands, never the left only. Pointing at someone with the left hand would also be considered improper.

WRITTEN AFRICAN LANGUAGES

Many of the African languages had no written form of any kind before missionaries lived with the tribes who spoke them. Missionaries often became linguists not because of an interest in language for its own sake but because they wanted to bring the Bible to the African people, and the most efficient way to do that was to translate it into the local languages. So they learned the African languages, some learning tens of languages. They then created written forms by transcribing them into the Roman alphabet.

Even today missionary societies keep vast databases of the African languages detailing where they are spoken, how many people speak them, and if they can be understood by other ethnic groups.

The Beja, a Muslim nomadic people living in the Red Sea Hills, speak Bedawiya, a language that has no written form. It is spoken by about 1.8 million people, 5 percent of Sudan's population.

OTHER AFRICAN LANGUAGES

There are about a hundred African languages spoken in Sudan. They can be classified into groups based on certain similarities in grammar and structure but are mostly mutually incomprehensible. This gives us some indication of just how ancient African society is. The more unlike two languages from the same language family are, the longer the two must have been spoken in order for such differences to have evolved.

The thousand or so languages of Africa are divided into four major groups: Afro-Asiatic, Niger-Kordofanian, Nilo-Saharan, and Niger-Congo. Arabic belongs to the Hamito-Semitic branch of the Afro-Asiatic language family. Some of the languages spoken along the Red Sea coast of Sudan, including Bedawiya and Hausa, are also members of this language family. Hausa, a West African tongue, is spoken by about 489,000 people.

Most of the other African languages spoken in Sudan belong to a completely different group, the Nilo-Saharan family. Dinka, several Nuba languages, and Shilluk belong to this group. Some of these languages are mutually intelligible. For example, the language of the Fur people around Darfur is spoken by about 1 million people but can also be understood by speakers of Nyala, Laguri, and other languages spoken in the area.

The most widely spoken non-Arabic language is Dinka, which is spoken in the South as a mother tongue and a lingua franca. Dinka is spoken by about 3 million people and in certain areas is used unofficially in classrooms.

Opposite: **Missionary institutions taught English and also recorded many African languages.**

It has wide regional differences but can be understood by the Nuer, who have their own language and have migrated around Sudan.

LITERACY

Sudan has poor literacy levels. With its hundreds of mother tongues, Sudan has had many problems in improving the rate of literacy. The government's plan to use Arabic as a unifying language of instruction in the 1970s only made matters worse. Not only were the people illiterate in their mother tongues, but they were illiterate in Arabic too. Also, the years of civil war in Sudan did not help the literacy problem. Constant fighting and terrorizing from militants caused many schools to close down. On top of that, there are many internally displaced Sudanese who are continually on the move, which makes education even more difficult. The problem is particularly challenging for the linguistically diverse South. Aid agencies recognize this problem and have set up schools that teach in the local languages. English is also taught as one of the subjects. Sudan also has to overcome the mindset that girls should be trained in domestic work and not educated.

Today 72 percent of men and 42 percent of women are able to read, compared with a decade ago when the literacy rates for men and women were 45 percent and 18 percent respectively.

There are about 273 television sets in Sudan for every thousand people. However, the numbers are disproportionately higher in towns and cities than in rural areas.

THE MEDIA

Before all privately owned newspapers were nationalized in 1970, Sudan had a large number of local and national newspapers. Political parties published a wealth of periodicals, and in Khartoum alone 22 daily papers were published—19 papers in Arabic and 3 in English. In all, Sudan had 55 daily or weekly newspapers and magazines. The media have since had a difficult time in Sudan, as each successive coup changed the direction of government. There are a few privately owned publications allowed today, and all publications are subjected to government censorship. Some examples of privately owned publications are the newspapers *Al-Ra'y al-Amm* (AHL-ra AHL-ahm), *Al-Khartoum*, and the English-language *Khartoum Monitor*. There are three other daily newspapers in Arabic: *El Ayaam* (EL EYE-ahm), *El Sahafa* (EL sah-HAH-fah), and *Alwan* (AHL-one). The state also produces *Al-Anba* (AHL-ahn-ba), the English-language paper *Sudan Vision*, and an English-language magazine called *Sudanow*. The SPLA issues its own newspaper and journals.

THE POLITICS OF LANGUAGE

Like most other things in Sudan, language has become a political issue. As part of the government drive to Islamicize Sudan, great emphasis has been placed on the acquisition of Arabic. Most speakers of Arabic as a mother tongue are Muslim. Although some Muslims such as Nubians speak their own mother tongue, they also use Arabic, and the indigenous languages are expected to decline. In fact eight indigenous languages are already extinct.

In the South and in the Nuba Mountains, refusing to speak Arabic is a means of resistance. The Nuba, who have been under intense pressure to abandon their culture, have chosen to teach their own languages in their schools. The Nuba and many organizations such as Amnesty International believe that the tribe's very existence is under threat, and speaking Nuba languages is one way of ensuring its survival until better times.

As many as 80 percent of Sudanese in towns own a radio, but the percentage drops in the rural areas. Even so, many people have access to a radio for at least part of the day. Radio is therefore a more common medium for getting updates on news. The low literacy level also contributes to the fact that few people read the papers. The Sudan National Radio Corporation is state owned and airs programming in Arabic, English, and some southern Sudan languages, offering a mixture of news, music, and cultural programs. People can also tune in to the Voice of America, Paris-based Radio Monte Carlo, and the BBC World Service. Opposition radio stations such as the Voice of Sudan from the National Democratic Alliance and the Voice of Freedom and Renewal from the Sudan Alliance Forces can also be heard broadcasting via shortwave in Arabic and English.

Television is a rare luxury owned by the wealthy few and by some of the richer social clubs. Satellite dishes are a common sight in affluent areas. The one television station, Sudan National Broadcasting Corporation (SNBC), is government owned. There are no privately owned television stations bar a cable service jointly owned by the government and private investors. SNBC has a permanent military censor to ensure that news aired reflects official views. SNBC broadcasts 60 hours of programming a week, and a typical night's viewing consists of news broadcasts, farming information, religious programs, commercials, and lastly entertainment, which makes up about half of the broadcasting time.

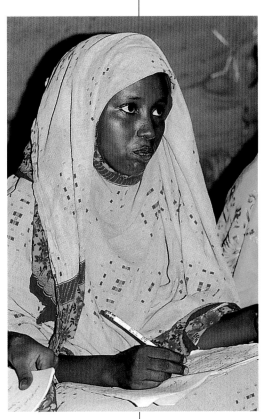

Literacy classes teach reading and writing to adults who missed out on early schooling.

ARTS

SUDAN HAS BEEN HOME to civilized life for thousands of years. Its cultural heritage goes back to the civilizations of ancient Egypt, Kerma, and Meroë, which produced complex architecture and artwork. At Musawwarat, es-Sufra is an interesting excavation of a huge Meroitic building named the Great Enclosure, with long, wide corridors, ramps, mazes, and rooms. Some archaeologists have suggested that the building was used as a pilgrimage center or a royal palace.

Sudan has produced musicians and artists from both its African and its Arabic traditions. Fine-arts students in Khartoum often put on displays of their work. That colleges of fine arts are still operating in Sudan is a sign of hope for the country.

Opposite: **Engravings on the Lion Temple built during the Meroe period.**

LIBRARIES AND MUSEUMS

Sudan has about 10 major libraries; two of the larger libraries are at the University of Khartoum and the Ahfad University for Women, with an estimated 800,000 books. Other libraries include the Institute of Education, with about 28,000 volumes, and the Khartoum Polytechnic, with a collection of 30,000 books. Minor libraries are maintained by secondary schools, places of worship, government agencies, and foreign community centers. There are six museums,

most of them in Khartoum. The National Museum (*pictured here*), in the center of the city, has two floors depicting the ancient history of Sudan, with displays of the remains of the ancient Kush civilization and rescued frescoes from the early churches. In the garden of the museum are reconstructed temples of Buhen and Semna, salvaged during the construction of the Aswan Dam. The Temple of Buhen dates back to 1490 B.C. and was built by the Egyptian queen Hatshepsut. Another ethnographic museum in Khartoum, which has since closed, was dedicated to artifacts of village life, many of which are still in use in parts of the country.

These small pyramids hold the bodies of Meroitian rulers.

ANCIENT ART AND ARCHITECTURE

One of the earlier sites of ancient architecture is Meroë, on the east bank of the Nile north of Khartoum. Meroë has many structures with Egyptian and Greco–Roman architectural influences, including the luxurious Royal City, dating back to the fourth century B.C., which is built inside an area of about 0.4 square miles (1 square km). It is a walled city, within which is another walled area, believed to be the palace. The buildings, which are of sandstone and mud brick and often faced with fired and glazed bricks, included audience chambers, shops, and temples. Most interesting, though, was an ornately decorated pool with a complex set of channels bringing water into it from a nearby well. About 3 miles (5 km) to the east of the desert stand the royal pyramids where the past kings of Meroë are buried.

Iron objects and pottery of a high quality have been found at many sites. The pottery was thrown on a potter's wheel, decorated, and fired.

Many of the items are considered among the finest pottery objects found in Africa. Remains of textiles prove that cotton was grown and made into cloth here at a very early stage. There are still thousands of sites yet to be fully excavated in Sudan. The most recent significant find was by a group of archaeologists from the University of Geneva in Switzerland. In Kerma, south of the Third Cataract of the Nile, a pit was found filled with large monuments and finely carved statues of seven Nubian kings. These granite statues, 4–10 feet (1.2–3.1 m) tall, are highly polished, finely carved, and engraved with the name of the king on the back and feet of each sculpture.

Smaller, more easily moved archaeological finds have been moved to several museums throughout Sudan.

A detailed fresco (wall painting) from the ancient cathedral at Faras.

EARLY CHRISTIAN ART AND ARCHITECTURE

Coptic Christian culture dominated the Middle Nile from about the sixth century A.D. to the eighth century A.D. Northern Sudan had several major cities where the commercial, political, and social life was highly complex and structured. Many churches were in good condition when they were abandoned, and over the centuries they have filled with windblown sand. The remains of three cathedrals and at least a hundred churches dating from the fourth century to the 15th century have been found. The earlier buildings are bigger and grander than the later ones, suggesting that Christianity declined during this period.

Churches had huge stone supporting columns and brick-lined vaults. There are remains of cathedrals at Old Dongola, Faras, and Qasr Ibrim. In the cathedral at Faras wall paintings of a high artistic quality have been preserved in the desert for hundreds of years. The paintings depict biblical scenes, Nubian kings, and high government officials.

In some sites gold and glass lamps have been discovered, along with gold and silver jewelry set with precious stones. Further evidence indicates that gold and architectural stone were mined or excavated in Sudan and either used in the country or traded abroad.

MODERN ARCHITECTURE

Just as in ancient times, architecture today says much about the spiritual and aesthetic life of a country. Modern Sudan's architectural masterpieces are its cathedrals and mosques. In Khartoum the most interesting mosque is the Two Niles Mosque, which stands at the confluence of the Blue Nile and the White Nile. Opened in 1984, it is a huge dome-shape geometrical building, standing out stark and white against the browns and reds of the desert. Conical patterns around its base remind the observer of the many memorials to holy men that

The distinctive dome of the Two Niles Mosque in Khartoum.

are scattered throughout the country. Another Khartoum mosque, built by King Farouk of Egypt, reflects a very different, almost colonial style of architecture. Its minaret and walls are ornately carved stone more in keeping with the architecture of colonial Khartoum.

At El Obeid is a large Catholic cathedral in which many aspects of African culture come together. Smaller churches throughout Sudan are much simpler in design, in keeping with African architecture. They are simple wooden or mud-walled buildings with straw roofs, which like most other African architecture will eventually disappear, leaving no evidence of their existence.

Sudanese women carrying handmade baskets to sell in the market. Traditional crafts like basket-weaving are practical and yet provide a source of income for the Sudanese.

ARTS AND CRAFTS

Craft work is still an important element in daily Sudanese life. In the West crafts have become an expensive rarity, but in Sudan everyday objects are handmade using ancient techniques. Domestic objects are woven using palm leaves or grasses, and complex woodcarving is still in evidence. The goods carved range from small, simple household items to large, elaborately decorated tables and beds. In Port Sudan, now quite rundown since Sudanese exports have declined, the older buildings still display elegant latticework in their window frames and doorways. In nearby Suakin the crumbling buildings show elegant architecture made from coral stone, which is gradually being eroded by the desert winds.

Crafts workers producing objects in gold, silver, and brass can be found in any souk in Sudan. Some ethnic groups wear exquisite silver and gold jewelry or carry ornate decorative swords, daggers, and knives, all of which one can see being made in the marketplace. The Azandes are particularly known for their expertise in making daggers such as the *shongo* (SHOWN-go), a multiblade throwing knife that spins as it flies, and a similarly lethal sickle-shape knife. Elaborate leather goods are made by the nomadic tribes to barter for food. The Baggara women are particularly famous for their elaborately patterned leather blankets adorned with cowry shells. Many of the southern tribes wear ornate necklaces made from ivory and precious stones. For the small tourist industry there are many carvings in ebony and other precious woods.

LITERATURE

Sudan has an ancient tradition of storytelling. Some stories told around firesides in Sudan have existed in one form or another for centuries. Many of the languages of Sudan had no written form until the missionaries began to transcribe them, so history and legends were handed down from one generation to another in an oral tradition.

In modern times men and women have found a voice in Sudanese society by retelling some of the ancient tales and creating new ones to record the lifestyles of the Sudanese. One modern Sudanese writer is Tayeb Saleh, who writes fictionalized accounts of the life of Sudanese people. His books include *The Wedding of Zein and Other Stories* and his best-known work, *The Season of Migration to the North,* both of which were published in the United States in 1978. His most recent work, *Bandarshah,* was published in 2003. Other writers include the controversially outspoken feminist Kola Boof and poets Taban Lo Liyong, Akol Meyan Kuol, and Leila Aboulela.

SUDANESE MUSICIANS

Abdel Gadir Salim, Abdel Aziz el Mubarak, Wardi, Hamza al–Din, and Mohamed Gubara are popular Sudanese musicians whose music has been brought to the West through albums and performances.

Salim fronts a small ensemble of oud, tabla (a kind of drum), and accordion, highlighting the rhythms and melodies as well as the voice of the artist. He also plays with a larger band.

Mubarak sings with oud, drum, and accordion. His influences are broader than Salim's, with traces of many other cultures slipping into his more urban interpretation. Gubara plays with a tambour. His sharper vocal style and sparse accompaniment create stunning music with an almost chilling intensity and energy.

Other contemporary Sudanese musicians include drummer Mahmoud Fadl; Emmanuel Jal, who sings in English, Swahili, Arabic, and the languages of the Dinka and the Nuer; Wafir, who is considered a virtuoso on the accordion, the violin, and the oud; and Hassouna Bangladish, who plays traditional Sudanese music with a contemporary feel.

MUSIC

The people of Africa have used percussion and string instruments as part of their religious worship and daily life for centuries, and the Sudanese are no exception. Many types of instruments, such as the drum known as the tambour among the Nubian and the *rababa* (RA-bah-bah), a stringed instrument, can be heard at religious celebrations and tribal dances.

The Dinka record all their activities, especially wars, initiations, and other major life events, in song. Through their songs the people can reinforce their identity, recall their ancestors, praise their group, or settle a dispute. Because they enshrine the history, beliefs, and values of the Dinka, many of their songs are about their all-important cattle.

The popular music of the North is influenced by the sounds, language, and instruments of Arabic culture. Khartoum and Omdurman have recording facilities that are accessible to rising talents as well as to established masters, and the wealth of popular music is disseminated through radio and inexpensive cassettes.

The oud is a musical instrument dating back to ancient Egypt. It is the most important musical instrument in Arab culture and is regarded as the forerunner of the European lute. It usually has five strings and is played with a plectrum or with the fingers of both hands.

LEISURE

WAR, FAMINE, AND POVERTY have hit some areas of Sudan harder than others, so the opportunity for leisure varies. In some areas life goes on pretty much as it always has. In the bigger towns and cities people spend the mornings working, while the afternoons are usually a time for resting until it is cooler. In the evenings, after offices close at 8 P.M., most men relax in one of the many clubs organized by religious, trade, or ethnic associations. The clubs usually serve food and nonalcoholic drinks, provide lectures or sporting activities such as squash, and occasionally have a television set or even show a movie. Card games are also popular.

Attending a club is less common for women. Women usually stay at home in the evening, prepare the evening meal, and perhaps, if they are wealthy, watch some local and satellite television.

Left: **Even in a harsh environment, children still find ways to have fun.**

Opposite: **The Sudanese often escape the heat of the afternoon by having a leisurely chat in the shade.**

Men playing cards in the village of Dalgo in Upper Nubia. Simple pleasures such as gathering with friends for a card game and chatting are popular with the Sudanese.

DAILY LEISURE

Outside the clubs, most towns are empty, dark places after sundown. However, there are an increasing number of restaurants, a number of movie theaters, and more street lighting. Many of the nightlife activities common in the West, however, are disapproved of. This was not the case before the declaration of shariah law. Khartoum had a reputation as a "fast" town with all kinds of nightlife and bars that sold local and imported alcohol. There are still illegal drinking clubs selling home-brewed and distilled drinks.

In the long hot afternoons, for those who do not sleep, there are many tea shops to visit to hear the latest gossip or to read the daily paper. In many societies shopping has become a leisure activity. To some extent this is true in Sudan. People go to shopping malls and the souk, which is liveliest in the early morning and where mostly men or older women go to do each day's shopping. In some towns there are newly arrived nomadic groups from Darfur and Kordofan with gossip from their last port of call or new shipments of scarce goods to look over. People can be seen meeting up at the Camel Market, west of Khartoum.

SPORTS

A very popular sport in Sudan is football (soccer) of the kind played in Europe. There is a national league, and some towns have two or more teams. The major sporting clubs in Khartoum are the Hilal Capitals, the Shabab Mirrikh, and the Morada. The Hilal Capitals often top the football league. Where there is a television, European matches are watched avidly.

Sudanese children play football (soccer) in the desert.

Wrestling is a famous tradition among the Nuba. This activity contributed to the Nuba's problems when they became a major tourist attraction in the 1970s and early 1980s. The Muslim government decided that the naked wrestling and dancing was irreligious, and the campaign to clothe and "civilize" the Nuba began. It is still possible to see Nuba wrestling on most Fridays in the Haj Yusef district of Khartoum North.

Sudan has always been a country where fine horses were bred, and Khartoum has a racecourse that is patronized by many of its citizens. Races are held on Fridays and Sundays, and polo matches are held on Wednesdays and Saturdays.

Other than their passion for football, most Sudanese have little time or money for sports. Some sports are organized in expatriate settlements that spring up as groups of aid workers arrive. Some settlements have a swimming pool; others have table tennis and other activities to keep the workers occupied. The expatriate community is biggest in Khartoum and is organized around national clubs.

A group of Dinka children entertain themselves.

LEISURE TO SUDANESE CHILDREN

Children in the West have a lot of leisure time, but for many children in Sudan games have to take second place to survival. Most rural children work alongside their mothers in the fields if they are not in school, and many spend a large part of each day traveling to and from the nearest source of water. Children as young as five are left in charge of their younger brothers and sisters. Dinka children spend their days in charge of their animals. When children do have leisure time it is spent perhaps in finding a use for pieces of scrap metal, bending them into the shapes of toys to sell to other people, or making kites from sticks and old plastic welded together with a burning cigarette.

In the aftermath of the war, some aid workers in southern Sudan formed drama groups and organized sports such as soccer and volleyball to help the children resocialize while participating in leisure activities.

STORYTELLING

One traditional activity that survives in Sudan is storytelling. Stories are passed on from older generations to the young. The Sudanese of the South share many of the folk stories of other areas of Africa, such as the stories of Ananse the spider—a story that also came to America with the Africans taken into slavery in the 18th and 19th centuries.

Other stories concern ghosts or history. In eastern Sudan there is a town called Suakin, which means "land of the genie." Suakin was said to be the home of a powerful genie. One legend tells how the queen of one of the tribes of Yemen sent a ship carrying seven virgin girls to King Solomon in Jerusalem. When the ship arrived in Jerusalem all the girls were expecting babies. The ship had been driven to Suakin by a storm, and all the girls had had affairs with the genie!

The Sudanese have lots of ghost stories to tell. One modern story tells of a tree outside an old prison in Kassala that was used to hang criminals. Local people believed that the suffering spirits of those executed lived in the tree. The tree died and was cut down to be used for firewood, but no one in the village would touch it. When a passing traveler took some of the wood and lit a fire he heard the voices of the dead people calling out to him from the flames.

Full Internet services were introduced to Sudan in 1997. Currently there are 16 Internet hosts in the country, with more than 2.8 million users.

FESTIVALS

DESPITE THEIR HARDSHIPS, people continue celebrating the important festivals of their lives. Sudan has three major religious groups: Muslim, Christian, and animist. The major Muslim festivals and Christmas Day coincide with public holidays. Other major public holidays are January 1, which celebrates Sudanese independence; March 3, Unity Day; and June 30, Revolution Day, commemorating the 1989 National Islamic Front military coup over the democratically elected government of former prime minister Sayyid Sadiq al-Mahdi.

MUSLIM FESTIVALS

There are two major religious festivals for Sudanese Muslims: Eid al-Fitr (EED AHL-fitr), which marks the end of Ramadan, and Eid al-Adha (EED AHL-ad-ah), which commemorates Abraham's being asked to sacrifice his son. Another day that many children look forward to is the Prophet

Left: **Music plays an important part in many Sudanese festivals.**

Opposite: **A Dinka girl undergoes the traditional scarring ceremony that marks her coming of age. Thin, superficial cuts are made and an irritant is rubbed on so that keloids would form.**

115

With an estimated 70 percent of Sudanese as Muslims, the most celebrated festivals are Islamic ones.

THE ISLAMIC CALENDAR

The solar calendar used in most of the world is known as the Gregorian calendar. It divides the year into a number of fixed days and months, with an extra day being added every four years (leap year) to allow for the difference between the calendar year of 365 days and the actual time it takes for the earth to circle the sun (which is just a little longer). Most Christian festivals, with the important exception of Easter, are based on this Gregorian solar calendar. Christmas Day is always December 25, and New Year's Day is always January 1.

Most Muslim festivals are based on the moon's rotation around the earth, following a lunar calendar. There are still 12 months, of either 29 or 30 days, but the lunar year is 10 or 11 days shorter than the Gregorian solar year. As a result, Muslim festivals are not held on the same date of the Gregorian calendar each year; it takes 33 years for a complete lunar-calendar cycle.

Muhammad's birthday, Maulid an-Nabi (MAU-lid an-nah-bee). Other Islamic celebrations include Laylat al-Qadar (LEE-lat AHL-ka-dar), celebrating the night of the first revelation of the Koranic verses to Muhammad; Israwal Miraj (is-RAH wal ME-raj), commemorating the Prophet's night journey from Mecca to Jerusalem and his ascension to establish the five pillars of the Islamic faith; and Muharram (moo-HAR-rahm), commemorating the martyrdom of Prophet Muhammad's grandson, Hussein, who was killed in battle.

EID AL-FITR During Ramadan, the month of fasting, the breaking of the fast each day occurs at the moment of dusk. Each evening becomes a feast as the family settles down to enjoy the success of another day's fasting. Eid al-Fitr, which begins on the first day of the 10th month, marks the end of Ramadan. Not surprisingly, it is characterized by feasting during the day. From a religious point of view, Eid al-Fitr signifies the glorious culmination of a period of spiritual cleansing and purification.

THE *ZAR* CEREMONY

Many women spend long periods of their life in the home, so festivals are often an occasion for women to go out and mix more freely than usual. The *zar* ceremony is just such an opportunity. It is held to help women who may be emotionally troubled. The ceremony is thought to soothe the spirits that possess them.

The highlight of the ceremony is a dance where women beat out a rhythm with drums and rattles, and troubled women get to their feet to dance to the music. A woman might have a particular object or talisman associated with the spirit that troubles her, and she will dance holding this object. The ceremony sometimes lasts as long as seven days.

THE *ZIKR* CEREMONY

This Muslim ceremony is regularly performed in the bigger towns of northern Sudan. The men who take part in the ceremony are known as whirling dervishes. They believe that through the rhythm and movement of dance they can gain a personal state of rapture and so commune with God. The men, wearing long white *jallabiya* and turbans, meet near a holy place, which is usually the grave of a holy person. The holy men who conduct the ceremony wear traditional colorful patched clothes.

Men move to the rhythm of drums, and from time to time one will break away from the crowd and whirl himself into a state of religious ecstasy. Young boys practice the dance at the outskirts of the crowd, and the occasional woman may join in, much to the disapproval of the men. The ceremony takes place on Friday evenings as dusk approaches and continues until night has fallen. In Omdurman this ceremony has become a tourist attraction.

Eid al-Fitr is the most festive period of the year for Sudanese Muslims. It is celebrated with large family meals that all members of an extended family will try to attend. Toward the end of Ramadan, the family home will be thoroughly cleaned in preparation. If there is money for new clothes or new furniture, this is the time when the shopping will be done. During the four days of celebration people wear their new clothes and visit friends and relatives. Eid al-Fitr is a cross between Thanksgiving and Christmas, being a religious, family, and social festival. Children receive gifts at this time of the year.

EID AL-ADHA This festival commemorates Abraham's willingness to sacrifice his son for God. It is also celebrated to mark the end of the hajj pilgrimage to Mecca. Muslims who can afford it sacrifice a sheep on the feast day and give a portion of the meat to the poor.

CHRISTIAN FESTIVALS

Christian festivals are still an important part of daily life in Sudan. Catholics celebrate the coming of Christmas with midnight Mass. Christmas Day is a public holiday, so families in the city spend the day together. Christians give gifts and eat a special Christmas lunch—a Sudanese feast rather than the traditional Western lunch. Easter is also celebrated, although it is not a public holiday.

ANIMIST FESTIVALS

Animist festivals are usually associated with the cycles of nature, such as harvests, changes of the seasons, the rise and fall of the Nile, and the coming of rain. The Shilluk have two major festivals, the rain dance and the harvest festival. Both festivals involve dance and offerings to the ancestors. They and the Dinka also have fishing festivals where hundreds of men go into the river in the Sudd to catch as many fish as possible.

ANIMAL SACRIFICE Many animist tribes practice animal sacrifice. To celebrate a special day (or to ward off danger or illness) the Dinka and Nuer tribes will sacrifice one of their cattle. They believe that performing the ritual brings a benevolent spiritual presence to the occasion. The ritual sacrifice involves long speeches and many gestures with the spear, and when the animal is slaughtered it is shared among the whole community according to strict laws of division. The ritual itself, rather than the death of the animal, is most important; if the Nuer have no ox available, they will substitute a nonedible cucumber and perform the rites in exactly the same way, even calling the cucumber "ox."

The Dinka spear-fishing festival.

FOOD

ALL TRAVELERS TO SUDAN agree that the Sudanese people, poor as they are, are among the most hospitable in the world. Travelers tell stories of how all over Sudan they were welcomed into people's homes and invited to share their food. Sudanese people have experienced the worst extremes of poverty and hardship, and yet Sudanese hospitality remains the same.

Throughout Sudan an important dish is *ful* (FOOL), made of cooked beans and often served with raw onions. In villages along the Nile or along a truck route, there are luxuries such as lentils and okra to add to the *ful*. Rice, sorghum, and millet are the staple grains. Sudanese eat flat Arabic bread and their own variety of bread called *kisra* (KISS-rah), a pancakelike unleavened bread made from sorghum.

Salt is a rare commodity and is bought in precious little packets from the market.

Left: **A Sudanese man bakes flat bread in Akuem village, Southern Sudan.**

Opposite: **A man does his shopping in ash-Shamaliyah state, Sudan. Due to the higher cost, most Sudanese do not shop in supermarkets or stores like this.**

FRESH INGREDIENTS

In the desert regions vegetables and fresh fruit are a rare luxury, and *ful* with *kisra* may be the only things people eat for weeks on end. In the South, where it rains regularly, there are citrus fruits and many varieties of vegetables to make a varied and interesting diet.

Meat consumption is common all over Sudan. However, because of the high cost and short storage life of meat, Sudanese find ways to extent the meat's shelf life. One way the Sudanese preserve meat is to dry it, cut it into strips, and then add the strips to stews. Favorite meats are lamb and chicken. Many people eat fish caught from the Nile or the lakes in the mountains. Fish is often eaten for breakfast.

There is very little processed food or refrigeration in rural areas, so most food is bought fresh daily from the souk. Some fruits and food are only seasonally available.

ALCOHOL

Fresh vegetables are available in this market in Nyala.

Under shariah law alcohol is forbidden to all citizens of Sudan, but illegal brews are made in remote areas and enjoyed by many people. *Aragi* (ah-rah-gi) is distilled from dates and is a little like white rum. In other areas *tedj* (TAY-dj), a wine made from fermented honey, is preferred. A beer called *merissa* (mer-EE-sah) is brewed from sorghum. It is easily available in the South.

EATING HABITS

Most Sudanese start their day with a cup of very sweet milky tea called *shai bi laban* (SHY bee LA-bahn). Throughout the cities and small towns and at intervals along all routes there are women with simple tea-making equipment ready to serve this breakfast staple.

The first meal of the day comes after the first of the morning's work, at around 9:30. For the better-off this is often a dish with liver, such as cooked liver with *ful* and fish, or raw lungs and liver served with hot chili. *Kibda* (KEEB-da), a dish of fried chopped liver, is a popular breakfast food. A second meal is eaten in the evening and might be vegetable stew with *ful*, salad, and if the family can afford it, a piece of mutton or beef. In the evening a drink of hot sweetened milk called *laban* (LA-bahn) is popular. Often the milk is flavored with nutmeg.

Outdoor tea shops cater to travelers throughout Sudan. This one is at the bus station in

A SUDANESE FEAST

In a Muslim household, the right hand is always used to give and receive food.

As the guests arrive they are offered a cooling drink such as freshly squeezed citrus juice or *kerkadey* (KAYRK-ah-deh), made from the hibiscus flower and sweetened with sugar. The offering of drinks is a symbolic gesture welcoming the guests after their "long journey."

A Sudanese feast

After freshening up, the guests are taken to the dining room, which is decorated with peacock feathers. Men and women are served in separate areas. At the center of the dining room is a low table surrounded by large comfortable cushions. A pitcher containing water and a large bowl are brought in, and guests' hands are washed.

The meal begins with soup brought out already served in bowls carried on a huge aluminum or brass tray. Each guest is given a bowl, which is held in the left hand while a spoon is held in the right. When the guests have finished they return the bowl and the spoon to the tray, which is then taken away.

The next tray carries the five or six remaining dishes of the meal, including *kisra*, which is used to scoop up the sauces. The host serves each person a piece of bread and a bowl of salad, and guests help themselves to food from the other dishes. Chili is served in little individual bowls. Food is eaten with a spoon or the right hand.

The hand-washing ritual is carried out again after the main course, and then dessert is served. There are very few cooked Sudanese desserts. Usually fresh fruit is peeled and served in segments, but there are a few more complicated dishes, such as a dessert very similar to crème caramel.

In northern Sudan there is a very special way of brewing coffee, called jebena (djah-BEE-nah) Sudaniya. *The coffee beans are fried over charcoal in a special pot and then ground with cloves and spices. The coffee is steeped in hot water, strained through a fresh grass sieve, and served in tiny coffee cups.*

THE FEAST MENU

For a very special occasion an animal will be slaughtered. The menu might be *shorba*, a soup sometimes made from pureed lamb; *mashi*, tomatoes and eggplants stuffed with rice and minced lamb; *gammonia*, stewed sheep's stomach, served with tomatoes and onions; a salad of tomatoes, lettuce, onions, and green peppers with a lime-juice dressing; *shata*, a little bowl of hot chili to add to the dishes; *kisra*; fresh fruit segments; and coffee.

FOOD

After the food, *jebena* coffee is served. This is named after the pot in which it is prepared. If guests prefer, they can have *qahwa bi habahan* (KAH-wa bee HA-ba-han), which is sweet hot coffee spiced with cardamom.

Finally the guests relax around the table while an incense burner filled with sandalwood is brought into the room to perfume the air.

During the month of Ramadan, breaking fast together at the end of the day is an important ritual for Muslim families.

TABOOS

The Islamic rules regarding which foods are "clean" apply in Sudan, where the majority of people are Muslim. Pork is not eaten in Muslim households (except among the Nuba, who believe that it is acceptable to eat pork and also to drink alcohol). Muslim law also prohibits eating shellfish, but this is not commonly available in Sudan anyway. Muslims eat only with the right hand, believing that the left hand is unclean as it is used strictly for bathroom ablutions.

KITCHENS AND UTENSILS

Because Sudan is one of the hottest countries in the world, most traditional or rural cooking takes place outside the house.

In more rural areas houses are one-room mud-walled huts with roofs of straw. Cooking is done outside over an open fire, which is often set in a hollow in the ground, with low mud walls around the sides. Balanced on the mud walls is a huge woklike metal pot in which thick vegetable and meat stews are boiled. The fire is fueled with kindling collected from the bush. Cooking utensils, spoons, cups, and plates are made from natural products, such as gourds, large leaves, or wood from the date palm.

In the countryside, there is little running water—water is stored in animal skins, in pottery jars, or in oil drums to which wheels have been

Beja girls cook sorghum porridge in the Red Sea province.

added to make the trips to the well easier. In some places the trunks of baobab trees are hollowed out and waterproofed with pitch to serve as water tanks.

Nomadic cooking facilities are quite similar except that they are small enough to be packed away and moved. In the desert there is less firewood to be found, so cooking is done very carefully using animal dung as fuel. In many areas of Sudan the ash from this type of fire is used as an effective mosquito repellent. Animal skins are used to store water and

A nomad collects wood for cooking. Because most of the Sudanese use wood for cooking, the number of trees and plants are rapidly depleted, leading to desertification.

to make tents, and cooking implements may be made of bone. Rather than growing all their own food, the nomads must visit towns to barter goods for fresh vegetables and enough sorghum and beans to last until their next visit to a town.

City kitchens are a little more sophisticated, but poorer people still cook outdoors over charcoal stoves. Many dishes such as meat kebabs and grilled liver are cooked directly over the coals, like a Western barbecue. There is piped water in some areas, although it is generally untreated water piped straight from the river. People have to boil their drinking water to kill the parasites that live in it. Plastic and metal kitchen utensils are bought from the souk.

For many women whose husbands have been lost in the civil war or have gone in search of work, brewing and selling tea or alcohol is their only means of making a living.

POPULAR FOOD IN SUDAN

Food in Sudan varies from one ethnic group to another. Differences in lifestyles and climates account for the types of food favored by a particular region. Northern Sudan is known for its simple wheat-based cuisine. The staple dish, *gourrassa* (GOO-rahs-sa), is made of wheat flour and baked into a circular shape. In eastern Sudan, the Ethiopian-influenced banana-paste dish called *moukhbaza* (MOOK-bah-za) is very popular. In the nomadic west, milk and dairy products are commonplace and are used in most of the cooking. The western region is also known for its cereal called *dukhun* (DOO-koon), which is used as a base for preparing thick porridges and stews. Central Sudan has a popular fish dish cooked with onions, spices, and tomato sauce called *fassikh* (FAS-sikh). Because vegetables and fish are more abundant in the South, the region is well known for its fish stew called *kajaik* (KA-jay-eek), which is usually eaten with *aseeda* (AH-see-da), which is a porridge made of sorghum.

MASHI (STUFFED TOMATOES WITH MEAT)

2 pounds (907 g) chopped beef
   or lamb
$1^1/_2$ teaspoons salt
$^1/_2$ teaspoon pepper
2 teaspoons garlic powder or
   4 cloves of garlic, mashed
4 tablespoons fresh dill, chopped
4 tablespoons olive oil
1 cup cooked rice
8 firm tomatoes or small eggplants
2 tablespoons butter
2 six-ounce (180 ml) cans
   tomato paste
2 six-ounce (180 ml) cans water
1 teaspoon cinnamon

In a bowl, thoroughly mix the beef, one teaspoon of salt, pepper, one teaspoon of garlic powder, and dill. Sauté the mixture in two tablespoons of oil until it browns. Add rice to the mixture, and stir well. Slit the tomatoes (or eggplants) halfway across the center, and carefully squeeze the sides to open them. With a spoon, scoop the seeds out. Fill the cavities of the tomatoes with the beef mixture. In a large skillet, melt the butter in two tablespoons of oil. Add the tomatoes and sauté them until they turn dark red on all sides. In another bowl mix the tomato paste, water, $^1/_2$ teaspoon of salt, cinnamon, and one teaspoon of garlic powder. Pour the tomato sauce over the tomatoes in the pan. Over a low flame, let the tomatoes cook for another 10-15 minutes. Then place the cooked tomatoes on a plate and serve. This recipe serves four to eight people.

CRÉME CARAMELA (SUDANESE CARAMEL CUSTARD)

8 eggs
4 cups milk
1 cup sugar
1 ounce (30 ml) melted butter
1 tablespoon vanilla extract
Maraschino or candied cherries (optional)

In a bowl, beat the eggs together with the milk and a half-cup of sugar until the mixture is frothy. Then add butter and vanilla to the mixture. Heat the remaining half-cup of sugar in a pan until it caramelizes. Pour the caramel into a cake pan, coating the bottom of the pan well. Beat the egg mixture once more, and quickly pour the mixture into the coated pan. Butter one side of a piece of aluminum foil. Cover the pan with the foil, buttered side facing the custard mixture. Then place the custard-filled pan in a larger pan half-filled with water. Bake for 30 minutes at 350°F (175°C). Remove the aluminum cover, and with a fork or a blunt knife poke once into the custard. If the fork or knife comes out clean, the custard is ready. Chill the custard thoroughly, then serve on a platter. If preferred, garnish the custard with the cherries.This recipe serves three.

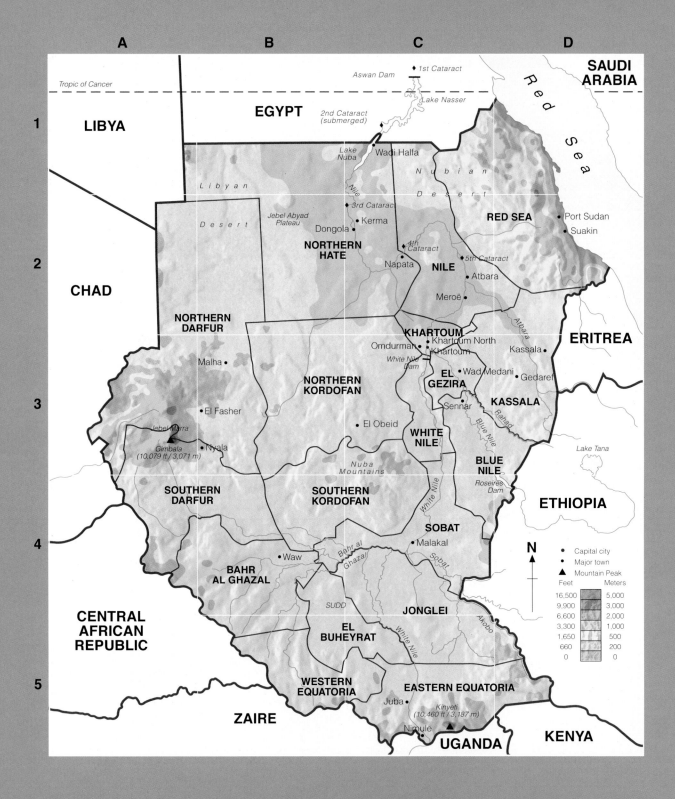

MAP OF SUDAN

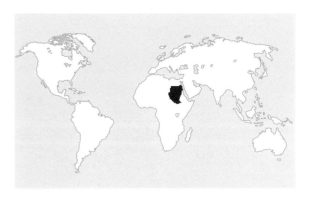

ECONOMIC SUDAN

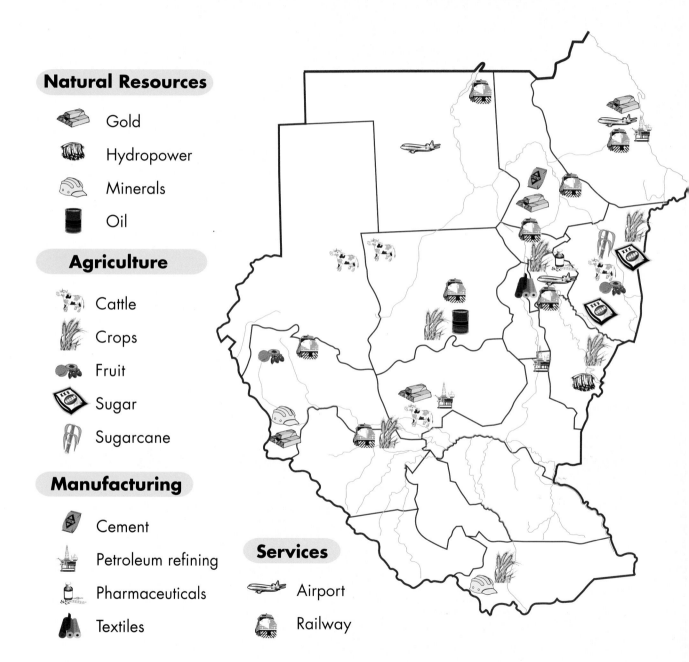

Natural Resources

- Gold
- Hydropower
- Minerals
- Oil

Agriculture

- Cattle
- Crops
- Fruit
- Sugar
- Sugarcane

Manufacturing

- Cement
- Petroleum refining
- Pharmaceuticals
- Textiles

Services

- Airport
- Railway

ABOUT THE ECONOMY

OVERVIEW

Sudan has been on the receiving end of considerable foreign investments and aid programs in the past. However, few of these funded projects have been realized, as Sudan suffers from chronic instability, mismanagement that includes huge international debts, drought, and weak world agricultural prices. Sudan has begun exporting crude oil, which has contributed immensely to its export earnings. For a few years now, Sudan has been improving its monetary policies and infrastructure investment. This was most evident in 2004, when Sudan maintained its GDP growth of 8.6 percent.

GROSS DOMESTIC PRODUCT (GDP)

$97.5 billion (2006 estimate)

GDP Growth

9.6 percent (2006 estimate)

LAND USE

Arable land: 6.78 percent; permanent crops: 0.17 percent; others: 93.05 percent (2005 estimates)

CURRENCY

1 Sudanese dinar (SDD) = 100 piastres
Notes: 5,000, 2,000, 1,000, 500, 200, 100, 50 SDD
Coins: 50, 20, 10, 5, 2, 1 piastres
USD1 = SDD 213.135 (2007)

NATURAL RESOURCES

Petroleum, small reserves of chromium ore, copper, gold, hydropower, iron ore, mica, silver, tungsten, zinc

AGRICULTURAL PRODUCTS

Banana, cotton, groundnut, gum arabic, mango, millet, papaya, sesame, sorghum, sugarcane, sweet potato, tapioca, wheat

INDUSTRIES

Armaments, automobile assembly, cement, cotton ginning, edible oil, oil, petroleum refining, pharmaceuticals, sugar, soap distilling, shoes, textiles

MAJOR EXPORTS

Oil and petroleum products, cotton, livestock, groundnut, gum arabic, sesame, sugar

MAJOR IMPORTS

Foodstuff, manufactured goods, medicine and chemicals, refinery and transport equipment, textiles, wheat

MAJOR TRADING PARTNERS

China, Japan, Saudi Arabia, UAE, Egypt, India (2005 estimates)

WORK FORCE

7.5 million (1996 estimate)

INFLATION RATE

9 percent (2006 estimate)

CULTURAL SUDAN

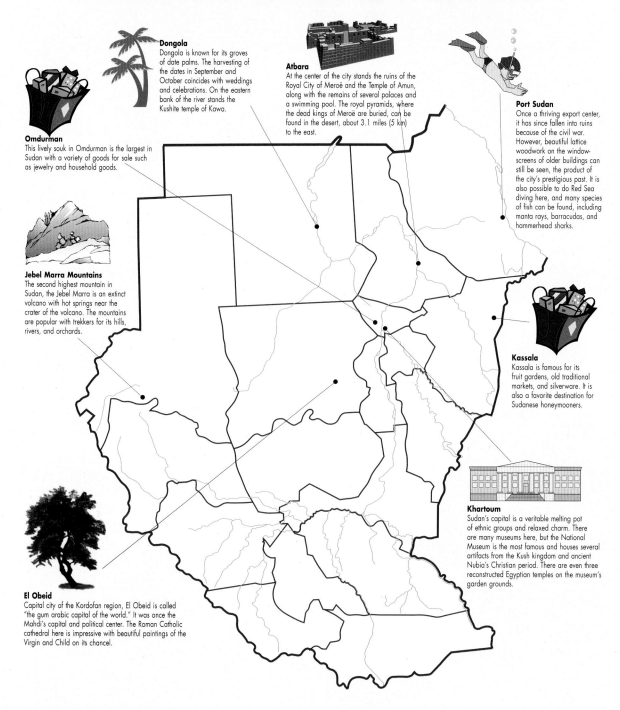

Dongola
Dongola is known for its groves of date palms. The harvesting of the dates in September and October coincides with weddings and celebrations. On the eastern bank of the river stands the Kushite temple of Kawa.

Atbara
At the center of the city stands the ruins of the Royal City of Meroë and the Temple of Amun, along with the remains of several palaces and a swimming pool. The royal pyramids, where the dead kings of Meroë are buried, can be found in the desert, about 3.1 miles (5 km) to the east.

Port Sudan
Once a thriving export center, it has since fallen into ruins because of the civil war. However, beautiful lattice woodwork on the window-screens of older buildings can still be seen, the product of the city's prestigious past. It is also possible to do Red Sea diving here, and many species of fish can be found, including manta rays, barracudas, and hammerhead sharks.

Omdurman
This lively souk in Omdurman is the largest in Sudan with a variety of goods for sale such as jewelry and household goods.

Jebel Marra Mountains
The second highest mountain in Sudan, the Jebel Marra is an extinct volcano with hot springs near the crater of the volcano. The mountains are popular with trekkers for its hills, rivers, and orchards.

Kassala
Kassala is famous for its fruit gardens, old traditional markets, and silverware. It is also a favorite destination for Sudanese honeymooners.

Khartoum
Sudan's capital is a veritable melting pot of ethnic groups and relaxed charm. There are many museums here, but the National Museum is the most famous and houses several artifacts from the Kush kingdom and ancient Nubia's Christian period. There are even three reconstructed Egyptian temples on the museum's garden grounds.

El Obeid
Capital city of the Kordofan region, El Obeid is called "the gum arabic capital of the world." It was once the Mahdi's capital and political center. The Roman Catholic cathedral here is impressive with beautiful paintings of the Virgin and Child on its chancel.

ABOUT THE CULTURE

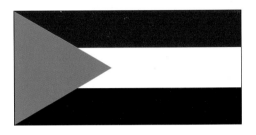

OFFICIAL NAME
Jamhuriyat as-Sudan (Republic of the Sudan)

FLAG DESCRIPTION
Three equal horizontal bands of red (on top), white, and black with a green isosceles triangle on the hoist side

CAPITAL
Khartoum

POPULATION
39,400,000 (2007 estimate)

RELIGIOUS GROUPS
Sunni Muslim: 70 percent; indigenous beliefs: 25 percent; Christian: 5 percent

ETHNIC GROUPS
Non-Arab: 52 percent; Arab: 39 percent; Beja: 6 percent; foreigners: 2 percent; other: 1 percent

BIRTHRATE
34.86 births per 1,000 Sudanese (2007 estimate)

DEATH RATE
14.39 deaths per 1,000 Sudanese (2007 estimate)

LITERACY RATE
61.1 percent (2003 estimate)

MAIN LANGUAGES
Arabic (official), Nubian, Tu Bedawin, diverse dialects of Nilotic and Nilo-Hamitic Sudanic languages, English

NATIONAL HOLIDAYS
Independence Day (January 1), Eid al-Adha (date varies), Islamic New Year (date varies), Unity Day (March 3), Uprising Day (April 6), Prophet Muhammad's Birthday (date varies), May Revolution Anniversary (May 25), Revolution Day (June 30), Eid al-Fitr (date varies), Christmas (December 25)

LEADERS IN POLITICS
Ibrahim Abbud—first president of independent Sudan (1958–64)
Jaafar al-Nimeiry—president of military government of Sudan (1969–85)
Sayyid Sadiq al-Mahdi—current leader of Umma Party. Prime minister of coalition government of Sudan (1966–67 and 1986–89)
Omar Hassan al-Bashir—president and prime minister of Sudan (1989–present)
John Garang—late Dinka leader and founder/leader of SPLA (1983–2005) and first vice president of Sudan (July 2005)
Salva Kiir—vice president of Sudan and leader of SPLA (2005–present); president of Southern Sudan

TIME LINE

IN SUDAN	IN THE WORLD
1504-1821 Funj kingdom, the largest of the Arab sultanates, controls central Sudan.	
	1530 Beginning of transatlantic slave trade organized by the Portuguese in Africa
1821 Egypt conquers the Funj kingdom.	**1861** The U.S. Civil War begins.
1877 The British and the Turks establish their authority in the region.	
1881–85 Muhammad Ahmad, the Mahdi, leads a revolt against Egypt and captures Khartoum.	
1885–98 Reign of the Mahdi and Khalifa Abdullahi.	
1898–99 British and Egyptian forces invade Sudan and begin Anglo-Egyptian rule.	**1914** World War I begins. **1939** World War II begins.
1953–55 Sudan is granted self-government by Britain and Egypt. Political conflict between the North and the South begins.	
1956 Sudan becomes an independent republic.	**1957** The Russians launch Sputnik.
1958 First military coup against the civilian government. General Ibrahim Abbud becomes president.	
1964 The October Revolution. General Abbud is overthrown. National democratic government is established.	**1966–69** The Chinese Cultural Revolution
1969 A second military coup brings Colonel Jaafar al-Nimeiry to power. He is "elected" president.	
1972 Al-Nimeiry signs a peace agreement giving the South autonomous regional government.	
1983 Al-Nimeiry imposes shariah law, leading to a new breakout of civil war in the South.	

IN SUDAN	IN THE WORLD
1985	
Al-Nimeiry is overthrown by a military coup.	
1986	**1986**
A coalition government is formed, with Sayyid Sadiq al-Mahdi elected as prime minister.	Nuclear power disaster at Chernobyl in Ukraine
1989	
Brigadier General Omar Hassan al-Bashir overthrows the al-Mahdi government.	**1991**
1996	Breakup of the Soviet Union
The South boycotts the general elections, and al-Bashir is "elected" president.	**1997**
1998	Hong Kong is returned to China.
The United States bombs a pharmaceutical plant in Khartoum. A new constitution is endorsed in Sudan.	
1999	
The president dissolves the National Assembly and declares a state of emergency.	
2000	
Al-Bashir is "reelected."	
2001	**2001**
Peace talks between al-Bashir and Garang fail.	Terrorists crash planes in New York, Washington, DC, and Pennsylvania.
2002	
Machakos Protocol signed to end civil war.	
2003	**2003**
Rebels in western region of Darfur rise up against the government.	War in Iraq begins.
2004	
Systematic killings in African villages in Darfur continue.	
2005	
Peace treaty for southern Sudan is finalized. Garang is sworn in as vice president. He dies not long after and is succeeded by Salva Kiir.	
2006	
Khartoum government and the main rebel faction in Darfur sign a peace accord. Two smaller rebel groups reject the move. Conflict in Darfur continues.	

GLOSSARY

araqi (AR-raki)
An alcoholic drink made from dates

faki (FAY-ki)
Folk Islamic soothsayers and religious scholars who practice traditional medicine across western Sudan

ful (FOOL)
A dish made from cooked beans

haboob (ha-BOOB)
A sudden sandstorm that occurs in central and northern Sudan

hashab (HASH-ab)
A dessert made of chopped bananas, figs, and raisins

imma (EM-ah)
An Arab man's turban

jallabiya (CHAL-a-bee-ah)
A loose cotton shirt worn by Arab men

jihad
To strive for individual spiritual perfection or to wage war against enemies of Islam

kisra (KISS-rah)
Sudanese unleavened bread, made from sorghum

lingua franca
A common language used by groups of people who speak different languages

mahdi
A Muslim religious leader or savior

muezzin
Mosque official who calls worshippers to pray five times daily

oud
Musical instrument with five strings, the forerunner of the lute, played with plectrum or fingers

Ramadan
The ninth month of the Islamic calendar, when Muslims must refrain from eating or drinking between dawn and dusk

shariah law
Islamic law, introduced throughout Sudan as state law by President al-Nimeiry in 1983

shorba (SHOR-bah)
A soup common in northern Sudan

souk
The city or village market

tobe (TOH-bay)
A long piece of thin fabric worn by many women in northern Sudan over clothes to cover the head and the body

FURTHER INFORMATION

BOOKS

Dalton, David. *Living in a Refugee Camp: Carbino's Story*. Milwaukee, WI: World Almanac Library, 2006.

DiPiazza, Francesca Davis. *Sudan in Pictures*. Minnesota, MN: Twenty-First Century Books, 2006.

Freeman, Michael. *Sudan: The Land and The People*. London: Thames & Hudson, 2005.

Holt, Peter Malcolm. *A History of the Sudan: From the Coming of Islam to the Present Day*. New York: Longman, 2000.

Hughes, Christopher. *Sudan*. Detroit, MI: Blackbirch Press, 2006.

Peterson, Scott. *Me Against My Brother*. New York: Routledge, 2000.

Petterson, Donald. *Inside Sudan: Political Islam, Conflict, and Catastrophe*. Boulder, CO: Westview Press, 2003.

Saleh, Tayeb. *The Season of Migration to the North*. Washington, DC: Three Continents Press, 1980.

Scroggins, Deborah. *Emma's War*. New York: Pantheon Books, 2002.

Smith, Wilbur. *The Triumph of the Sun: A Novel of African Adventure*. London: Pan, 2006.

WEB SITES

1A1: Sudan Page. www.sudan.net

Central Intelligence Agency World Factbook (select Sudan from country list). www.cia.gov/cia/publications/factbook

Darfur Information Center. www.darfurinfo.org

International Crisis Group. www.crisisweb.org

Lonely Planet World Guide: Sudan. www.lonelyplanet.com/worldguide/destinations/africa/sudan

Nuba Mountains. www.nubamountains.com

Sudan Studies Association. www.sudanstudies.org

FILM

All About Darfur. Taghreed Elsanhouri Productions, 2005

Insan (Human Being). Arab Film Distribution, 1994.

Lost Boys of Sudan. Actual Films, 2003.

The Remembering Ground. 710 Main Productions, 2005.

MUSIC

The Rough Guide to the Music of Sudan. World Music Network, 2005.

BIBLIOGRAPHY

Asher, Michael. *A Desert Dies*. New York, St. Martin's Press, 1987.

Lonely Planet Guide to Egypt and Sudan. Melbourne: Lonely Planet Publications, 1988.

Voll, John Obert and Sarah Potter Voll. *The Sudan: Unity and Diversity in a Multicultural State*. Boulder, CO: Westview Press, 1985.

The Bradt Travel Guide: Sudan. Guilford, CT: Globe Pequot Press, 2005.

Embassy of the Republic of the Sudan. www.sudanembassy.org

The Republic of the Sudan Ministry of Foreign Affairs. www.sudanmfa.com

Sudan Information Gateway. www.sudanig.org

Sudan Tribune. www.sudantribune.com

INDEX